MW00699247

PLAY WITH THE DAY

Yearly goal journal to help you cast a vision, set monthly
intentions and live with soul.

A Soul Scroll Journal
By Suzanne Heyn

*We help you know, love and trust yourself
to create a life as unique as you are.*

This is the journal of:

_____

Documenting the year of:

_____

© Copyright 2019 Suzanne Heyn

All content is original by Suzanne Heyn. All rights reserved.

Cover, layout and design by Soul Scroll Journals.

No part of this book may be reproduced, scanned or distributed in any printed or electronic form without permission.

For more information, visit SoulScrollJournals.com or email hello@soulscrolljournals.com.

You can also learn more about Suzanne's work at SuzanneHeyn.com.

DISCLAIMER

This book is for entertainment purposes only. This journal is not a substitute for therapy or professional medical or mental health advice.

Although the Author has made every effort to ensure the information in this book was correct at press time, the author does not assume and hereby disclaims any liability to any part for any loss, damage, or disruption caused by this book.

The Author and/or distributors are not responsible for any adverse effects resulting from the use of the suggestions outlined in this program.

Table of contents

Welcome!

Hello beautiful dreamer! I am so excited you're here. This yearly goal journal is different than most planners, and I wanted to take a moment and explain the intention behind it.

This journal is designed to help you live a soulful life, with intention, love and joy. A life of enjoying the present moment while steadfastly creating your dreams and goals.

Living this way allows you to co-create magical things with the intelligence of the universe rather than achieve things by logic alone. It allows you to live by flow rather than force.

Many planners and people focus on managing time, but what we really need to manage is energy. The right action done at the right time takes way less time, with a better result. This is the essence of living from flow.

And when you follow the flow, while connected to your bigger vision to make sure you're flowing in the right direction, you're always guided to do the exact perfect thing at the exact perfect time.

Living this way is impossible to schedule. It requires trust, the habit of continually checking in to your higher self, and of consistently reconnecting to your vision and intention.

This is what you'll learn how to do through working with this journal.

Living with soul is about balancing structure, held in place through self-care rituals and healthy habits, with a willingness to flow with your soul's guidance in the moments between. The result is an extraordinary life, one as unique as you are.

With good habits firmly in place — and connected to what you want to create and who you want to become — you have a solid foundation on which to flow.

This means following your soul's moment-by-moment guidance, including right next steps or inspired actions that come from seemingly nowhere. This is the kind of guidance society tells us to ignore, but that the world's most successful people have found the courage to follow.

You might receive a crazy idea no-one else thinks will work but you. You might be guided to do something seemingly unimportant, like take a pottery class.

You may even be guided to go get a massage, watch a movie, or take a hike rather than do the work you were supposed to get done.

In the old paradigm, following our instincts like this was viewed as flaky or flighty. Sometimes it might look like slacking. But what if on your walk, or while leaving yoga, you received a fantastic idea that infused a brand new, electric energy into your project? What if in your pottery class you met someone who became a great friend?

Of course it's important to sit down and do the work. It's important to be grounded enough to sit with a single project until completion and to honor the commitments you make to yourself. That's what habits and rituals and a bigger vision are all about.

But we have to leave room for magic. We have to leave room to change our minds.

When you live by a list or rigidly follow plans that don't feel good or don't seem to be working simply because it's written in your calendar, you're much more likely to quit your goals or become trapped in a life that doesn't bring you joy.

You're also relegating yourself to achieving your goals the normal way, the logical way, by brute force alone, and missing out on the incredible co-creative manifestation powers of the universe that are always feeding you with inspired guidance to achieve the seemingly impossible — as long as it's in your highest good!

You create this kind of life moment by moment, when you allow yourself to be guided.

Things change. Phases of life and parts of ourselves die, and the projects, plans and sometimes people or places associated with those parts must fall away from our lives so new things can be born. Even a habit or ritual that once felt good might suddenly feel heavy. You'll know then it's time to shift.

Allow yourself this grace. Know when you're in resistance, but also know when to let go, or to shift to accommodate changing needs.

If this way of living is totally new to you, no worries. You'll soon see the more you allow yourself to be guided, the louder and more clear this guidance will become.

We have to trust ourselves enough to rely on our visions, and know that our inner guidance is always directing us forward on the best path toward realizing those visions, even if we don't always understand what's happening.

That said, it's important to balance this flowy, feminine energy with masculine structure! When it comes to projects, that means breaking things down into little pieces, and scheduling each piece out. That's why I've included space to do that in this journal. But it's not the sole purpose or intention.

The main purpose and intention of this journal is to connect you to your vision and goals, to help you trust yourself, to learn the habit of checking in and receiving the inner guidance to move forward. It's to help you live from the heart rather than the head.

The purpose is also to help you focus on a few precious goals at a time so you may manifest beautiful things without stress or damaging your wellbeing.

Know that the universe and your higher self is always, always orchestrating the exact perfect external situations to guide you.

Get in the habit of looking at your surroundings, looking for the signs, for the guidance, and then trusting the process enough to flow with it. Go with it.

Even if it's not on your list or schedule for the day. Especially then.

May the next 12 months be full of magic and synchronicities. May all your dreams come true. And most importantly — may you love yourself and life along the way.

All the love,

Suzanne Heyn

Founder Soul Scroll Journals

PS — Share your journaling rituals on social media tagging #soulscrolling or @soulscrolljournals for the chance to be featured!

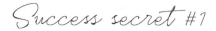

Welcome to this journey of shifting from the mind to the heart!

The mind likes to plan, analyze, strategize and worry. That's what it does! This is actually a survival mechanism. The mind tries to figure out everything that could possibly go wrong so it can protect you. This is useful, but also a source of suffering and anxiety.

The truth is, it's impossible to create the perfect plan for the perfect result. Life hardly ever goes to plan!

Living from the heart is about staying connected to your desire, idea or project emotionally. Your desires and projects have a life and intelligence to them. They evolve and grow just as you do.

Every time you take a step, the one after that will become obvious. In this way, manifesting your dreams and creating projects becomes an adventure, a collaborative back-and-forth process with the universe.

This way is about sensing and responding more than planning and strategizing.

When you notice yourself over-planning, it can be helpful to make a list. Get everything down on paper. Also remind yourself — "I'm planning because I'm nervous." Ask yourself what you're afraid of. Usually our fears have nothing to do with the surface anxiety, but reflect some deeper fear of unworthiness.

Go deeper to uncover the truth with compassion. The more we can move from a place of worthiness and trust, the more magically our lives unfold.

Find a collection of free bonus journaling prompts, meditations and other resources to help you know, love and trust yourself so you can create a life as unique as you are at SoulScrollJournals.com/bonuses.

Part 1: Review

The first step to creating a beautiful vision for your life is to honestly but compassionately review how things are going.

This process will help you release things you no longer want or need, creating space for the things you do.

Reviewing the past isn't about beating yourself up, and it's certainly not about measuring where you are in life compared to where you think you should be.

Instead, this review is intended to help you create intention and awareness.

To create space between you and the noise and speed of daily life so you can see how things are going.

Think of this section as a check-in. An opportunity for your inner wisdom to weigh in and offer your conscious self guidance for the future.

How did this year go for you? Free write your thoughts and feelings.

_____

_____

_____

_____

_____

_____

_____

_____

_____

_____

_____

_____

_____

_____

_____

_____

_____

_____

_____

_____

_____

_____

What was your intention or goal at the beginning of the year? If you're not sure, where were you in life in January?

_____

_____

_____

_____

_____

_____

_____

_____

_____

_____

How did you do in honoring that intention or honoring yourself if you can't remember? (Please stay in a loving place with this inquiry. Just noticing. No judgment!)

_____

_____

_____

_____

_____

_____

_____

_____

_____

What obstacles or detours came up for you? How did you respond to them? How would you like to respond in the future? Consider everything from your attitude to your thoughts to behavioral responses.

_____

_____

_____

_____

_____

_____

_____

_____

_____

_____

_____

_____

_____

_____

_____

_____

_____

_____

_____

_____

_____

What was your biggest lesson this year?

_____

_____

_____

_____

_____

_____

_____

_____

_____

_____

What was the highlight or defining moment of the year? What do
you remember most fondly?

_____

_____

_____

_____

_____

_____

_____

_____

_____

What personal qualities, habits or commitments helped to create that defining moment? What inner resistance did you overcome? How can you create more of these positive moments in the future?

_____

_____

_____

_____

_____

_____

_____

_____

_____

_____

_____

_____

What qualities or lessons from this year do you want to keep going forward?

_____

_____

_____

_____

_____

_____

_____

_____

_____

_____

_____

_____

_____

_____

What are you ready to leave behind? What have you outgrown or doesn't fit the person you are becoming?

_____

_____

_____

_____

_____

_____

_____

_____

_____

_____

_____

_____

_____

_____

_____

What do you want to tell yourself as you close out the year? What message does your higher self have for you?

_____

_____

_____

_____

_____

_____

_____

_____

_____

_____

_____

_____

_____

_____

_____

_____

_____

_____

_____

_____

_____

You are exactly who you're supposed to be, and where you're supposed to be. You are doing a good job. You are here on purpose.

Part 2: Daydream

Before we dive into specific plans and goals for the year, take time to dream!

Allow the questions in this section to stir your inner fire. Write freely, uncensored. Take the whispers in your heart seriously. They're there for a reason!

Even if a nudge seems random or purposeless, every message in your heart contains the seed of something beautiful. You never know where following one of those seemingly random or crazy ideas will take you.

This isn't a time to be practical or reasonable or logical. Those ideas are just false limits that don't actually exist.

It's not a time to think about what your parents would say or what your significant other or friends would think.

And it isn't a time to be influenced by useless negative self-talk or what you think will impress other people.

This is time for you, to tune into your soul, to create space, and ask your heart: What do you want for yourself in life?

If there were no limits, what would you most want for yourself in life? What do you want your life to be about? What do you want to create or experience?

_____

_____

_____

_____

_____

_____

_____

_____

_____

_____

_____

_____

_____

_____

_____

_____

_____

_____

_____

_____

_____

_____

What type of person do you want to be or become? Include inner qualities or any worldly achievements that feel inspiring or exciting.

_____

_____

_____

_____

_____

_____

_____

_____

_____

_____

_____

_____

_____

_____

_____

_____

_____

_____

_____

_____

_____

_____

What's most important to you in life? What do you value and prioritize?

_____

_____

_____

_____

_____

_____

_____

_____

_____

What about these desires is meaningful to you? How will receiving what you desire positively impact your life and the lives of others?

_____

_____

_____

_____

_____

_____

_____

_____

_____

What qualities do you already inhabit that will be helpful for manifesting your bigger dreams?

_____

_____

_____

_____

_____

_____

_____

_____

_____

_____

_____

_____

Where in life do things not feel fully you? Where are you holding back, or what feels more stressful or forced than you'd like? Where do you feel anxious or not fully self-expressed?

_____

_____

_____

_____

_____

_____

_____

_____

_____

_____

_____

_____

_____

_____

_____

_____

If these areas shifted to include more confidence, flow, fulfillment and ease, what would that look like? What would you know to be true? How would your actions shift in response? What message does your soul have for you about this?

_____

_____

_____

_____

_____

_____

_____

_____

_____

_____

_____

_____

_____

_____

_____

_____

_____

_____

_____

_____

If you took such amazing care of yourself that you literally glowed, what would that look like? What self-care practices would you do? What would you no longer do?

_____

_____

_____

_____

_____

_____

_____

_____

_____

_____

_____

_____

If you stepped into the next level of self-confidence, what would be different in your life right now?

_____

_____

_____

_____

_____

_____

_____

_____

_____

_____

_____

_____

_____

_____

_____

_____

_____

_____

_____

_____

_____

_____

_____

What would make this next year really great? Placing yourself in next December and looking back on the 12 months that just passed, what are you feeling pleased about?

_____

_____

_____

_____

_____

_____

_____

_____

_____

_____

_____

_____

_____

_____

_____

_____

_____

_____

_____

_____

_____

Just keep showing up, and you'll be amazed at the things you can do.

Part 3: Cast a vision

Inside of your heart lies a beautiful vision. Manifesting this vision is your life's mission, should you choose to accept it. Walking towards this vision will grow you as you grow it.

While casting your vision, keep in mind that you're exactly where you're meant to be right now. You are good enough right now. You can find joy now. In fact, finding joy in your existing phase of life is the quickest way to expand into the next.

Your desires will never be satisfied because as long as you are alive, the beautiful fuel of wanting more will inspire you to create miraculous things, which in turn allows you to explore different facets of yourself.

This is exactly why it's important to have visions for each area of your life rather than neglecting certain things, thinking you'll attend to them once you get "there." There is no there. Life is now.

With that in mind, this section invites you to ponder your desires in eight key areas of life, connecting to a beautiful vision for each one. Ready? Let's go!

Main intention:

What do you most want for yourself this year? Think about things you might like to achieve or experience, but also how you want to grow as a person. What are your main intentions or goals?

_____

_____

_____

_____

_____

_____

_____

_____

_____

_____

_____

_____

_____

_____

_____

_____

_____

_____

_____

_____

_____

_____

MAIN INTENTION OR GOAL FOR 20___

Affirmations:

1. Spiritual practice and relationship with self:

What is your ideal spiritual practice? What is your relationship like to God / The Universe? How does it feel? Do you have any sacred rituals you like to do? How do you care for and nourish yourself? How do you feel about yourself? What thoughts and beliefs do you hold about yourself? How do you maintain positive beliefs? How do you maintain balance? What is your vision in this area for the next year?

VISION FOR SPIRITUAL PRACTICE AND RELATIONSHIP WITH SELF

Affirmations:

Next steps:

2. Body and health:

How do you feel in your body? What is your relationship to your body? How do you care for yourself and nurture your energy? How often do you exercise, and what type of exercise do you do? What kind of foods do you eat? How and when do you relax and restore? What is your vision in this area for the next year? If this is an area of stress or sadness for you, what do you need to know from your soul in order to heal? What does your body want to tell you?

_____

_____

_____

_____

_____

_____

_____

_____

_____

_____

_____

_____

_____

_____

_____

_____

_____

VISION FOR BODY AND HEALTH

Affirmations:

Next steps:

3. Home:

What is your ideal home like? How does it feel? What types of furnishings do you have? Where do you live? What kind of view do you have? Any special amenities that would feel really special to you? What changes would make your home right now feel amazing, if you are not living in your ideal home? What is your vision in this area for next year?

VISION FOR YOUR HOME

Affirmations:

Next steps:

4. Finances and money:

What is your ideal relationship to money? In what ways does money support you? How much do you receive each month or year? How does receiving this money feel? What do you use it for? What kinds of investments, if any, do you have? How would you love your experience of money to evolve over the coming year?

_____

_____

_____

_____

_____

_____

_____

_____

_____

_____

_____

_____

_____

_____

_____

_____

_____

_____

_____

VISION FOR FINANCES AND MONEY

Affirmations:

Next steps:

5. Relationships:

How do your relationships with your loved ones, including family and friends, feel? What kinds of things do you do together? Is there anything you no longer do? What do you give from the heart, with generosity? What are you no longer available for? What is your experience of friends or community like? If this is something you are wanting to build, what would that look like? What is your vision in this area for next year?

_____

_____

_____

_____

_____

_____

_____

_____

_____

_____

_____

_____

_____

_____

_____

_____

_____

VISION FOR RELATIONSHIPS

Affirmations:

Next steps:

6. Career:

How would you love your career to evolve over the next year?
What projects would you love to work on? If you're looking for a
new job or career, what would that look like? What is your ideal
schedule? What do you want your working environment to be
like? How do you want your work to feel? What do you want your
relationship with your clients / co-workers to feel like? How do
you want to be treated and thought of?

_____

_____

_____

_____

_____

_____

_____

_____

_____

_____

_____

_____

_____

_____

_____

_____

_____

_____

_____

VISION FOR CAREER

Affirmations:

Next steps:

7. Personal growth:

How do you love to grow intellectually, to feed your mind? Are there any big personal goals you want to achieve this year? Maybe you want to take a big trip, run an important race, read a book a month or hire a mentor. If not, how would you love to grow personally this year?

_____

_____

_____

_____

_____

_____

_____

_____

_____

_____

_____

_____

_____

_____

_____

_____

_____

_____

_____

VISION FOR PERSONAL GROWTH

Affirmations:

Next steps:

8. Hobbies, free time and fun:

What hobbies do you have? How do you spend your free time?
How much free time do you have? What kind of boundaries ensure
you have time for renewal and play? Is there anything you feel
called to start or explore in the coming year?

_____

_____

_____

_____

_____

_____

_____

_____

_____

_____

_____

_____

_____

_____

_____

_____

_____

_____

_____

VISION FOR HOBBIES, FREE TIME AND FUN

Affirmations:

Next steps:

Anything else?

_____

_____

_____

_____

_____

_____

_____

_____

_____

_____

_____

_____

_____

_____

_____

_____

_____

_____

_____

_____

_____

_____

_____

_____

_____

_____

_____

_____

VISION

Affirmations:

Next steps:

Part 4: Build a positive mindset

When creating changes in your life, it's important to be honest about your fears.

Boldly envisioning your dreams will automatically illuminate all your inner doubts and fears.

This is a good thing because these limitations have always been there, playing in the background and limiting your enjoyment of life. Now you get to free yourself and live the life you really want.

These fears aren't true, even if they feel true. They're simply things you picked up along the way.

The bigger truth is that your desires come straight from your soul, and the mere fact that you have these dreams proves you're worthy and capable.

You are a divine being of infinite potential, stardust sandwiched in skin. All doubt is, is an identification with your small self rather than your infinite self.

Whenever you feel afraid or doubtful, return to your breath. Return to your body. Return to yourself and remember who you are!

What are some fears you have about the future or your ability to realize your dreams?

_____

_____

_____

_____

_____

_____

_____

_____

_____

_____

_____

_____

_____

_____

_____

_____

_____

_____

_____

_____

_____

_____

_____

_____

Are these fears true? If they possibly are, what is the higher truth? There is always a more expanded truth. Anything that limits you isn't the ultimate truth. If you need help, create silence and ask for guidance. Write a new, more positive story.

Why do you NOT want to achieve your dreams? How is staying where you are in life keeping you safe? What are you afraid will happen if you make changes?

_____

_____

_____

_____

_____

_____

_____

_____

_____

_____

_____

_____

_____

_____

_____

_____

_____

_____

_____

_____

_____

_____

_____

How can you see this differently? What messages does the future you have for the current you? Create space to really connect to this future vision of you and allow her to speak to you.

What inner or outer obstacles usually arise when you're trying to create forward momentum? How will you overcome these obstacles? What kind of support do you want to surround yourself with? Are there any boundaries you need to set with self or others?

_____

_____

_____

_____

_____

_____

_____

_____

_____

_____

_____

_____

_____

_____

_____

_____

_____

_____

_____

_____

_____

_____

The version of you who is confident and clear, knows what she wants and knows she's gonna get it — how does she feel / think / act? What does she believe about herself? Channel her energy now and free write.

_____

_____

_____

_____

_____

_____

_____

_____

_____

_____

_____

_____

_____

_____

_____

_____

_____

_____

_____

_____

Part 5: Create stepping stones to your vision

The secret to realizing your dreams is simply to become the person for whom it's inevitable.

This means that rather than obsessing over how to realize your dreams, simply make success a habit. For example, don't think about writing a book. Think about writing for 30 minutes or 1,000 words each day.

The mind wants to keep us safe by running ahead, but the reality is that letting our thoughts run amok creates tension and anxiety. Living this way destroys the joy of creation. Too much mind disconnects us from the heart.

Following your heart is about taking one next right step at a time.

It's okay to start small and let little actions create momentum. I believe that's the most solid, soulful way to create change. Create one good habit. Fill your life with increasing pockets of joy. Keep adding to it.

One day you'll look up, and the visions you wrote in these pages will be real. You'll smile and marvel how it all happened so easily. Like magic.

Tune into the person you desire to be and some of the goals you just set. What are the top three or four non-negotiable habits or rituals you want to do daily? This could include fitness, journaling, reading, meditating, creative work, etc.

If you're currently far away from where you want to be, choose one thing to start, based on your highest intention at the moment, and build from there.

When will you do these habits? What needs to release in your mind or life to create space for them?

HOW TO USE THE
PLAY WITH THE DAY SYSTEM

Step 1:

Connect to a desired outcome or goal. (Let's use the example of writing a book.)

Step 2:

Allow this desire to inspire you, and from this place of inspiration, open up to receive ideas or next steps. Stay connected to this feeling. Let it guide you into action.

Step 3:

List necessary actions. Break everything into bite-sized pieces. (Outline the book, write the first draft of each chapter, edit each chapter.)

Step 4:

Schedule the action steps with mini deadlines. (Finish Chapter 1 by next Friday.)

Step 5:

Make daily effort a habit. (Write 1,000 words or for a specific amount of time. If you want to get fancy, divide your total word count for the entire chapter by the number of days allotted to finish it, and write that amount each day.)

Step 6:

Keep asking: "What's my next right step?," and follow any nudges or ideas that make you feel excited.

Part 6: live with soul

Here we go! This is not a regular planner, and it's not intended to help you track appointments or meetings.

Instead, it's intended to be a book that helps you stay close to your soul while following your dreams.

In these pages, you'll find space to set monthly intentions and goals, connect to action steps, and at the end, review how things went.

Goals can be specific, like signing 5 new clients, or they can be general, like getting your eating back on track.

Even if you don't know HOW to achieve a certain goal, what's most important is to identify it and sit with the desire every day — might make a nice morning ritual! — until you receive an action step from within. Then, take that step!

Revisit your vision often. Things change — don't feel tied to something if it no longer lights you up. But it's important to stay emotionally connected to the things you identify as meaningful rather than lose yourself in the noise.

You can create anything you dream of. It's my hope this journal be a bridge to help you do it.

January

INTENTIONS

What are you grateful for?

_____

_____

_____

What do you most desire?

_____

_____

_____

What is your main intention or goal for the month?

_____

What affirmations, beliefs or attitudes will help you achieve your goals?

_____

_____

_____

What message does your higher self have for you about this month or any challenges you're experiencing?

_____

_____

_____

_____

JANUARY GOALS

Goal #1:

_____

Why do you want this? What part does it play in your larger vision?

_____

_____

Imagine the outcome. How does it feel?

_____

What actions are involved? What is your right next step?

_____

_____

Schedule the actions. Take the steps. Make it a habit.

Goal #2:

_____

Why do you want this? What part does it play in your larger vision?

_____

_____

Imagine the outcome. How does it feel?

_____

What actions are involved? What is your right next step?

_____

_____

Goal #3:

_____

Why do you want this? What part does it play in your larger vision?

_____

_____

Imagine the outcome. How does it feel?

_____

What actions are involved? What is your right next step?

_____

_____

***

What will happen if you don't make these changes? What is the cost of inaction?

_____

_____

_____

_____

What doubts and fears are you having? What more positive thoughts can you remind yourself of when you feel doubtful or afraid?

_____

_____

_____

_____

JANUARY NEXT STEPS

S	M	T	W	Th	F	Sa

Intention:

Monthly goals   >>>   Rituals / habits / next steps

Hold the vision and take one next right step at a time.

JANUARY REVIEW

What went well? What would you like to celebrate?

_____

_____

_____

What challenges did you face? What did you learn from them?

_____

_____

_____

What would you like to work on or improve? Any new skills you want to learn?

_____

_____

_____

What is something you're ready to release?

_____

_____

_____

How are you feeling? Any shifts in life or self-care you feel called to make?

_____

_____

_____

Let repetition be your effort.

February
INTENTIONS

What are you grateful for?

_____

_____

_____

What do you most desire?

_____

_____

_____

What is your main intention or goal for the month?

_____

What affirmations, beliefs or attitudes will help you achieve your goals?

_____

_____

_____

What message does your higher self have for you about this month or any challenges you're experiencing?

_____

_____

_____

_____

FEBRUARY GOALS

Goal #1:

_____

Why do you want this? What part does it play in your larger vision?

_____

_____

Imagine the outcome. How does it feel?

_____

What actions are involved? What is your right next step?

_____

_____

Schedule the actions. Take the steps. Make it a habit.

Goal #2:

_____

Why do you want this? What part does it play in your larger vision?

_____

_____

Imagine the outcome. How does it feel?

_____

What actions are involved? What is your right next step?

_____

_____

Goal #3:

_____

Why do you want this? What part does it play in your larger vision?

_____

_____

Imagine the outcome. How does it feel?

_____

What actions are involved? What is your right next step?

_____

_____

***

What will happen if you don't make these changes? What is the cost of inaction?

_____

_____

_____

_____

What doubts and fears are you having? What more positive thoughts can you remind yourself of when you feel doubtful or afraid?

_____

_____

_____

_____

FEBRUARY NEXT STEPS

S	M	T	W	Th	F	Sa

Intention:

Monthly goals   >>>   Rituals / habits / next steps

It's okay if you don't know how your dream will manifest. Just keep following your heart, and it will all work out.

FEBRUARY REVIEW

What went well? What would you like to celebrate?

_____

_____

_____

What challenges did you face? What did you learn from them?

_____

_____

_____

What would you like to work on or improve? Any new skills you want to learn?

_____

_____

_____

What is something you're ready to release?

_____

_____

_____

How are you feeling? Any shifts in life or self-care you feel called to make?

_____

_____

_____

When things don't flow, maybe it's time to let something go.

March

INTENTIONS

What are you grateful for?

_____

_____

_____

What do you most desire?

_____

_____

_____

What is your main intention or goal for the month?

_____

What affirmations, beliefs or attitudes will help you achieve your goals?

_____

_____

_____

What message does your higher self have for you about this month or any challenges you're experiencing?

_____

_____

_____

_____

MARCH GOALS

Goal #1:

_____

Why do you want this? What part does it play in your larger vision?

_____

_____

Imagine the outcome. How does it feel?

_____

What actions are involved? What is your right next step?

_____

_____

Schedule the actions. Take the steps. Make it a habit.

Goal #2:

_____

Why do you want this? What part does it play in your larger vision?

_____

_____

Imagine the outcome. How does it feel?

_____

What actions are involved? What is your right next step?

_____

_____

Goal #3:

_____

Why do you want this? What part does it play in your larger vision?

_____

_____

Imagine the outcome. How does it feel?

_____

What actions are involved? What is your right next step?

_____

_____

***

What will happen if you don't make these changes? What is the cost of inaction?

_____

_____

_____

_____

What doubts and fears are you having? What more positive thoughts can you remind yourself of when you feel doubtful or afraid?

_____

_____

_____

_____

MARCH NEXT STEPS

S	M	T	W	Th	F	Sa

Intention:

Monthly goals   >>>   Rituals / habits / next steps

You are wildly talented and capable of anything.

MARCH REVIEW

What went well? What would you like to celebrate?

_____

_____

_____

What challenges did you face? What did you learn from them?

_____

_____

_____

What would you like to work on or improve? Any new skills you want to learn?

_____

_____

_____

What is something you're ready to release?

_____

_____

_____

How are you feeling? Any shifts in life or self-care you feel called to make?

_____

_____

_____

Love yourself now. Find joy in the now. There's no there, only now.

April

INTENTIONS

What are you grateful for?

_____

_____

_____

What do you most desire?

_____

_____

_____

What is your main intention or goal for the month?

_____

What affirmations, beliefs or attitudes will help you achieve your goals?

_____

_____

_____

What message does your higher self have for you about this month or any challenges you're experiencing?

_____

_____

_____

_____

APRIL GOALS

Goal #1:

_____

Why do you want this? What part does it play in your larger vision?

_____

_____

Imagine the outcome. How does it feel?

_____

What actions are involved? What is your right next step?

_____

_____

Schedule the actions. Take the steps. Make it a habit.

Goal #2:

_____

Why do you want this? What part does it play in your larger vision?

_____

_____

Imagine the outcome. How does it feel?

_____

What actions are involved? What is your right next step?

_____

_____

Goal #3:

_____

Why do you want this? What part does it play in your larger vision?

_____

_____

Imagine the outcome. How does it feel?

_____

What actions are involved? What is your right next step?

_____

_____

***

What will happen if you don't make these changes? What is the cost of inaction?

_____

_____

_____

_____

What doubts and fears are you having? What more positive thoughts can you remind yourself of when you feel doubtful or afraid?

_____

_____

_____

_____

APRIL NEXT STEPS

S	M	T	W	Th	F	Sa

Intention:

Monthly goals   >>>   Rituals / habits / next steps

You are always guided. Everything is always working out for the highest good.

APRIL REVIEW

What went well? What would you like to celebrate?

_____

_____

_____

What challenges did you face? What did you learn from them?

_____

_____

_____

What would you like to work on or improve? Any new skills you want to learn?

_____

_____

_____

What is something you're ready to release?

_____

_____

_____

How are you feeling? Any shifts in life or self-care you feel called to make?

_____

_____

_____

You have something nobody else has. Be brave enough to be you.

May

INTENTIONS

What are you grateful for?

_____

_____

_____

What do you most desire?

_____

_____

_____

What is your main intention or goal for the month?

_____

What affirmations, beliefs or attitudes will help you achieve your goals?

_____

_____

_____

What message does your higher self have for you about this month or any challenges you're experiencing?

_____

_____

_____

_____

MAY GOALS

Goal #1:

_____

Why do you want this? What part does it play in your larger vision?

_____

_____

Imagine the outcome. How does it feel?

_____

What actions are involved? What is your right next step?

_____

_____

Schedule the actions. Take the steps. Make it a habit.

Goal #2:

_____

Why do you want this? What part does it play in your larger vision?

_____

_____

Imagine the outcome. How does it feel?

_____

What actions are involved? What is your right next step?

_____

_____

Goal #3:

_____

Why do you want this? What part does it play in your larger vision?

_____

_____

Imagine the outcome. How does it feel?

_____

What actions are involved? What is your right next step?

_____

_____

***

What will happen if you don't make these changes? What is the cost of inaction?

_____

_____

_____

_____

What doubts and fears are you having? What more positive thoughts can you remind yourself of when you feel doubtful or afraid?

_____

_____

_____

_____

MAY NEXT STEPS

S	M	T	W	Th	F	Sa

Intention:

Monthly goals   >>>   Rituals / habits / next steps

Just keep adding beautiful things. That's how you create a beautiful life.

MAY REVIEW

What went well? What would you like to celebrate?

_____

_____

_____

What challenges did you face? What did you learn from them?

_____

_____

_____

What would you like to work on or improve? Any new skills you want to learn?

_____

_____

_____

What is something you're ready to release?

_____

_____

_____

How are you feeling? Any shifts in life or self-care you feel called to make?

_____

_____

_____

The secret to get where you want to go is to fully be where you are.

INTENTIONS

What are you grateful for?

What do you most desire?

What is your main intention or goal for the month?

What affirmations, beliefs or attitudes will help you achieve your goals?

What message does your higher self have for you about this month or any challenges you're experiencing?

JUNE GOALS

Goal #1:

_____

Why do you want this? What part does it play in your larger vision?

_____

_____

Imagine the outcome. How does it feel?

_____

What actions are involved? What is your right next step?

_____

_____

Schedule the actions. Take the steps. Make it a habit.

Goal #2:

_____

Why do you want this? What part does it play in your larger vision?

_____

_____

Imagine the outcome. How does it feel?

_____

What actions are involved? What is your right next step?

_____

_____

Goal #3:

_____

Why do you want this? What part does it play in your larger vision?

_____

_____

Imagine the outcome. How does it feel?

_____

What actions are involved? What is your right next step?

_____

_____

***

What will happen if you don't make these changes? What is the cost of inaction?

_____

_____

_____

_____

What doubts and fears are you having? What more positive thoughts can you remind yourself of when you feel doubtful or afraid?

_____

_____

_____

_____

JUNE NEXT STEPS

S	M	T	W	Th	F	Sa

Intention:

Monthly goals   >>>   Rituals / habits / next steps

Your value is not in what you do, but in who you are.

JUNE REVIEW

What went well? What would you like to celebrate?

_____

_____

_____

What challenges did you face? What did you learn from them?

_____

_____

_____

What would you like to work on or improve? Any new skills you want to learn?

_____

_____

_____

What is something you're ready to release?

_____

_____

_____

How are you feeling? Any shifts in life or self-care you feel called to make?

_____

_____

_____

Do it because you love it. If you don't love it, don't do it.

July

INTENTIONS

What are you grateful for?

_____

_____

_____

What do you most desire?

_____

_____

_____

What is your main intention or goal for the month?

_____

What affirmations, beliefs or attitudes will help you achieve your goals?

_____

_____

_____

What message does your higher self have for you about this month or any challenges you're experiencing?

_____

_____

_____

_____

JULY GOALS

Goal #1:

_____

Why do you want this? What part does it play in your larger vision?

_____

_____

Imagine the outcome. How does it feel?

_____

What actions are involved? What is your right next step?

_____

_____

Schedule the actions. Take the steps. Make it a habit.

Goal #2:

_____

Why do you want this? What part does it play in your larger vision?

_____

_____

Imagine the outcome. How does it feel?

_____

What actions are involved? What is your right next step?

_____

_____

Goal #3:

_____

Why do you want this? What part does it play in your larger vision?

_____

_____

Imagine the outcome. How does it feel?

_____

What actions are involved? What is your right next step?

_____

_____

***

What will happen if you don't make these changes? What is the cost of inaction?

_____

_____

_____

_____

What doubts and fears are you having? What more positive thoughts can you remind yourself of when you feel doubtful or afraid?

_____

_____

_____

_____

JULY NEXT STEPS

S	M	T	W	Th	F	Sa

Intention:

Monthly goals   >>>   Rituals / habits / next steps

You are good enough. You are worthy. You are doing a good job.

JULY REVIEW

What went well? What would you like to celebrate?

_____

_____

_____

What challenges did you face? What did you learn from them?

_____

_____

_____

What would you like to work on or improve? Any new skills you want to learn?

_____

_____

_____

What is something you're ready to release?

_____

_____

_____

How are you feeling? Any shifts in life or self-care you feel called to make?

_____

_____

_____

In tears of joy or sadness, let them flow. Each leads to the other.

August

INTENTIONS

What are you grateful for?

_____

_____

_____

What do you most desire?

_____

_____

_____

What is your main intention or goal for the month?

_____

What affirmations, beliefs or attitudes will help you achieve your goals?

_____

_____

_____

What message does your higher self have for you about this month or any challenges you're experiencing?

_____

_____

_____

_____

AUGUST GOALS

Goal #1:

_____

Why do you want this? What part does it play in your larger vision?

_____

_____

Imagine the outcome. How does it feel?

_____

What actions are involved? What is your right next step?

_____

_____

Schedule the actions. Take the steps. Make it a habit.

Goal #2:

_____

Why do you want this? What part does it play in your larger vision?

_____

_____

Imagine the outcome. How does it feel?

_____

What actions are involved? What is your right next step?

_____

_____

Goal #3:

_____

Why do you want this? What part does it play in your larger vision?

_____

_____

Imagine the outcome. How does it feel?

_____

What actions are involved? What is your right next step?

_____

_____

***

What will happen if you don't make these changes? What is the cost of inaction?

_____

_____

_____

_____

What doubts and fears are you having? What more positive thoughts can you remind yourself of when you feel doubtful or afraid?

_____

_____

_____

_____

AUGUST NEXT STEPS

S	M	T	W	Th	F	Sa

Intention:

Monthly goals   >>>   Rituals / habits / next steps

Following your dreams is a practice. Just keep showing up every day.

AUGUST REVIEW

What went well? What would you like to celebrate?

_____

_____

_____

What challenges did you face? What did you learn from them?

_____

_____

_____

What would you like to work on or improve? Any new skills you want to learn?

_____

_____

_____

What is something you're ready to release?

_____

_____

_____

How are you feeling? Any shifts in life or self-care you feel called to make?

_____

_____

_____

Soulfulness isn't about perfection, but beauty in the imperfection.

September
INTENTIONS

What are you grateful for?

_____

_____

_____

What do you most desire?

_____

_____

_____

What is your main intention or goal for the month?

_____

What affirmations, beliefs or attitudes will help you achieve your goals?

_____

_____

_____

What message does your higher self have for you about this month or any challenges you're experiencing?

_____

_____

_____

_____

SEPTEMBER GOALS

Goal #1:

_____

Why do you want this? What part does it play in your larger vision?

_____

_____

Imagine the outcome. How does it feel?

_____

What actions are involved? What is your right next step?

_____

_____

Schedule the actions. Take the steps. Make it a habit.

Goal #2:

_____

Why do you want this? What part does it play in your larger vision?

_____

_____

Imagine the outcome. How does it feel?

_____

What actions are involved? What is your right next step?

_____

_____

Goal #3:

_____

Why do you want this? What part does it play in your larger vision?

_____

_____

Imagine the outcome. How does it feel?

_____

What actions are involved? What is your right next step?

_____

_____

***

What will happen if you don't make these changes? What is the cost of inaction?

_____

_____

_____

_____

What doubts and fears are you having? What more positive thoughts can you remind yourself of when you feel doubtful or afraid?

_____

_____

_____

_____

SEPTEMBER NEXT STEPS

S	M	T	W	Th	F	Sa

Intention:

Monthly goals   >>>   Rituals / habits / next steps

Getting grounded is how you rise.

SEPTEMBER REVIEW

What went well? What would you like to celebrate?

_____

_____

_____

What challenges did you face? What did you learn from them?

_____

_____

_____

What would you like to work on or improve? Any new skills you want to learn?

_____

_____

_____

What is something you're ready to release?

_____

_____

_____

How are you feeling? Any shifts in life or self-care you feel called to make?

_____

_____

_____

Life isn't about anything other than the experience of being alive.

INTENTIONS

What are you grateful for?

_____

_____

_____

What do you most desire?

_____

_____

_____

What is your main intention or goal for the month?

_____

What affirmations, beliefs or attitudes will help you achieve your goals?

_____

_____

_____

What message does your higher self have for you about this month or any challenges you're experiencing?

_____

_____

_____

_____

OCTOBER GOALS

Goal #1:

_____

Why do you want this? What part does it play in your larger vision?

_____

_____

Imagine the outcome. How does it feel?

_____

What actions are involved? What is your right next step?

_____

_____

Schedule the actions. Take the steps. Make it a habit.

Goal #2:

_____

Why do you want this? What part does it play in your larger vision?

_____

_____

Imagine the outcome. How does it feel?

_____

What actions are involved? What is your right next step?

_____

_____

Goal #3:

_____

Why do you want this? What part does it play in your larger vision?

_____

_____

Imagine the outcome. How does it feel?

_____

What actions are involved? What is your right next step?

_____

_____

***

What will happen if you don't make these changes? What is the cost of inaction?

_____

_____

_____

_____

What doubts and fears are you having? What more positive thoughts can you remind yourself of when you feel doubtful or afraid?

_____

_____

_____

_____

OCTOBER NEXT STEPS

S	M	T	W	Th	F	Sa

Intention:

Monthly goals   >>>   Rituals / habits / next steps

You are perfect as you are. You are beautiful. You are wise!

OCTOBER REVIEW

What went well? What would you like to celebrate?

_____

_____

_____

What challenges did you face? What did you learn from them?

_____

_____

_____

What would you like to work on or improve? Any new skills you want to learn?

_____

_____

_____

What is something you're ready to release?

_____

_____

_____

How are you feeling? Any shifts in life or self-care you feel called to make?

_____

_____

_____

Your inner guidance knows more than any outsider or expert.

INTENTIONS

What are you grateful for?

_____

_____

_____

What do you most desire?

_____

_____

_____

What is your main intention or goal for the month?

_____

What affirmations, beliefs or attitudes will help you achieve your goals?

_____

_____

_____

What message does your higher self have for you about this month or any challenges you're experiencing?

_____

_____

_____

_____

NOVEMBER GOALS

Goal #1:

_____

Why do you want this? What part does it play in your larger vision?

_____

_____

Imagine the outcome. How does it feel?

_____

What actions are involved? What is your right next step?

_____

_____

Schedule the actions. Take the steps. Make it a habit.

Goal #2:

_____

Why do you want this? What part does it play in your larger vision?

_____

_____

Imagine the outcome. How does it feel?

_____

What actions are involved? What is your right next step?

_____

_____

Goal #3:

_____

Why do you want this? What part does it play in your larger vision?

_____

_____

Imagine the outcome. How does it feel?

_____

What actions are involved? What is your right next step?

_____

_____

***

What will happen if you don't make these changes? What is the cost of inaction?

_____

_____

_____

_____

What doubts and fears are you having? What more positive thoughts can you remind yourself of when you feel doubtful or afraid?

_____

_____

_____

_____

NOVEMBER NEXT STEPS

S	M	T	W	Th	F	Sa

Intention:

Monthly goals　　　>>>　　　Rituals / habits / next steps

It doesn't have to be perfect to be wonderful.

NOVEMBER REVIEW

What went well? What would you like to celebrate?

_____

_____

_____

What challenges did you face? What did you learn from them?

_____

_____

_____

What would you like to work on or improve? Any new skills you want to learn?

_____

_____

_____

What is something you're ready to release?

_____

_____

_____

How are you feeling? Any shifts in life or self-care you feel called to make?

_____

_____

_____

A good life is built on a foundation of good habits and self-care.

INTENTIONS

What are you grateful for?

_____

_____

_____

What do you most desire?

_____

_____

_____

What is your main intention or goal for the month?

_____

What affirmations, beliefs or attitudes will help you achieve your goals?

_____

_____

_____

What message does your higher self have for you about this month or any challenges you're experiencing?

_____

_____

_____

_____

DECEMBER GOALS

Goal #1:

_____

Why do you want this? What part does it play in your larger vision?

_____

_____

Imagine the outcome. How does it feel?

_____

What actions are involved? What is your right next step?

_____

_____

Schedule the actions. Take the steps. Make it a habit.

Goal #2:

_____

Why do you want this? What part does it play in your larger vision?

_____

_____

Imagine the outcome. How does it feel?

_____

What actions are involved? What is your right next step?

_____

_____

Goal #3:

_____

Why do you want this? What part does it play in your larger vision?

_____

_____

Imagine the outcome. How does it feel?

_____

What actions are involved? What is your right next step?

_____

_____

***

What will happen if you don't make these changes? What is the cost of inaction?

_____

_____

_____

_____

What doubts and fears are you having? What more positive thoughts can you remind yourself of when you feel doubtful or afraid?

_____

_____

_____

_____

DECEMBER NEXT STEPS

S	M	T	W	Th	F	Sa

Intention:

Monthly goals   >>>   Rituals / habits / next steps

*Loving and accepting everything exactly as it is, is the foundation
for beautiful change!*

DECEMBER REVIEW

What went well? What would you like to celebrate?

_____

_____

_____

What challenges did you face? What did you learn from them?

_____

_____

_____

What would you like to work on or improve? Any new skills you want to learn?

_____

_____

_____

What is something you're ready to release?

_____

_____

_____

How are you feeling? Any shifts in life or self-care you feel called to make?

_____

_____

_____

Celebrate all you are, all you've been, and all you've yet to become.

Ideas for daily habits and self-care rituals

*Morning spiritual practice. (Meditation, journaling, light a candle, drink warm lemon water. Whatever inspires you!)

*Daily dry brushing and oil massage, followed by a bath or shower morning or night.

*Chant a mantra for 40 days or do a 40-day yoga practice.

*30 day money mindset, gratitude or confidence practice.

*Take a walk, read a book or listen to a guided meditation during an afternoon break.

*Listen to positive affirmations while cooking or getting ready.

*Read 10 pages of a book each day.

*Spend 30 minutes each day playing an instrument or learning a new language.

*Care for your skin: Morning massage or nightly facial.

*Journal your thoughts and feelings or affirmations.

*Sip a cup of tea during a mindful pause as part of your day.

*Spend time working on a creative project or hobby.

Pick one new self-care habit and set the goal to do it daily for 30 days. After the 30 days, check in and see if you want to continue, add something else, or maybe try something new.

The secret to expanding your life is to add things that make you happy rather than worry about removing the things that don't.

The things that aren't good for you will naturally get crowded out as you focus on the things that are.

What you focus on expands. Focus on adding pockets of joy, and over time those pockets will overflow!

Focusing on one new habit at a time rather than trying to overhaul your life is very important for success. Add one new thing, make it a habit, and then add another.

This way you're creating a strong foundation that will support you to infinity and beyond.

And don't forget the most important part — have fun!

It's time to play with the day!

Part 7: Track your habits

The foundation of your life lies upon healthy habits and rituals. Habits keep you grounded and energized, maintain your health and focus, and help you balance structure and flow.

This habit tracker offers the exact layout I used to get back on track when all my healthy habits disappeared, and my life along with it.

Following this system has gifted me with renewed energy, vitality and zest for life. I hope it offers you the same.

The spread is intentionally designed to keep you focused on your monthly intention and support you in creating a weekly focus based on your goals.

Use the empty space for lists, notes, dreams, to display your monthly goals or even do a short weekly review. Whatever your heart feels called to express.

May this habit tracker help you artfully string together the days of your life. May it be the solid foundation that allows you to blossom into whatever you choose to create.

Weekly focus:

Sunday _____

AM Habits	Meals
_____ __	B: _____
_____ __	L: _____
_____ __	D:_____

Mid-Day Habits	Water
_____ __	☐ ☐ ☐ ☐
_____ __	☐ ☐ ☐ ☐
_____ __	

PM Habits	To Do's
_____ __	_____ __
_____ __	_____ __
_____ __	_____ __

Monday _____

AM Habits	Meals
_____ __	B: _____
_____ __	L: _____
_____ __	D:_____

Mid-Day Habits	Water
_____ __	☐ ☐ ☐ ☐
_____ __	☐ ☐ ☐ ☐
_____ __	

PM Habits	To Do's
_____ __	_____ __
_____ __	_____ __
_____ __	_____ __

Affirmation:

Tuesday _____

AM Habits	Meals
_____ __	B: _____
_____ __	L: _____
_____ __	D:_____

Mid-Day Habits	Water
_____ __	☐ ☐ ☐ ☐
_____ __	☐ ☐ ☐ ☐
_____ __	

PM Habits	To Do's
_____ __	_____ __
_____ __	_____ __
_____ __	_____ __

Wednesday _____

AM Habits	Meals
_____ __	B: _____
_____ __	L: _____
_____ __	D:_____

Mid-Day Habits	Water
_____ __	☐ ☐ ☐ ☐
_____ __	☐ ☐ ☐ ☐
_____ __	

PM Habits	To Do's
_____ __	_____ __
_____ __	_____ __
_____ __	_____ __

Monthly intention:

Thursday _____

AM Habits — Meals
_____ __   B: _____
_____ __   L: _____
_____ __   D: _____

Mid-Day Habits — Water
_____ __   ☐ ☐ ☐ ☐
_____ __   ☐ ☐ ☐ ☐

PM Habits — To Do's
_____ __   _____ __
_____ __   _____ __
_____ __   _____ __

Friday _____

AM Habits — Meals
_____ __   B: _____
_____ __   L: _____
_____ __   D: _____

Mid-Day Habits — Water
_____ __   ☐ ☐ ☐ ☐
_____ __   ☐ ☐ ☐ ☐

PM Habits — To Do's
_____ __   _____ __
_____ __   _____ __
_____ __   _____ __

Affirmation:

Saturday _____

AM Habits — Meals
_____ __   B: _____
_____ __   L: _____
_____ __   D: _____

Mid-Day Habits — Water
_____ __   ☐ ☐ ☐ ☐
_____ __   ☐ ☐ ☐ ☐

PM Habits — To Do's
_____ __   _____ __
_____ __   _____ __
_____ __   _____ __

Space to Clear Your Mind

Weekly focus:

Sunday _____

AM Habits | Meals
_____ __ | B: _____
_____ __ | L: _____
_____ __ | D:_____

Mid-Day Habits | Water
_____ __ | ☐ ☐ ☐ ☐
_____ __ | ☐ ☐ ☐ ☐

PM Habits | To Do's
_____ __ | _____ __
_____ __ | _____ __
_____ __ | _____ __

Monday _____

AM Habits | Meals
_____ __ | B: _____
_____ __ | L: _____
_____ __ | D:_____

Mid-Day Habits | Water
_____ __ | ☐ ☐ ☐ ☐
_____ __ | ☐ ☐ ☐ ☐

PM Habits | To Do's
_____ __ | _____ __
_____ __ | _____ __
_____ __ | _____ __

Affirmation:

Tuesday _____

AM Habits | Meals
_____ __ | B: _____
_____ __ | L: _____
_____ __ | D:_____

Mid-Day Habits | Water
_____ __ | ☐ ☐ ☐ ☐
_____ __ | ☐ ☐ ☐ ☐

PM Habits | To Do's
_____ __ | _____ __
_____ __ | _____ __
_____ __ | _____ __

Wednesday _____

AM Habits | Meals
_____ __ | B: _____
_____ __ | L: _____
_____ __ | D:_____

Mid-Day Habits | Water
_____ __ | ☐ ☐ ☐ ☐
_____ __ | ☐ ☐ ☐ ☐

PM Habits | To Do's
_____ __ | _____ __
_____ __ | _____ __
_____ __ | _____ __

Monthly intention:

Thursday _____

AM Habits   Meals

_____ __   B: _____

_____ __   L: _____

_____ __   D:_____

Mid-Day Habits   Water

_____ __   ☐ ☐ ☐ ☐

_____ __   ☐ ☐ ☐ ☐

_____ __

PM Habits   To Do's

_____ __   _____ __

_____ __   _____ __

_____ __   _____ __

Friday _____

AM Habits   Meals

_____ __   B: _____

_____ __   L: _____

_____ __   D:_____

Mid-Day Habits   Water

_____ __   ☐ ☐ ☐ ☐

_____ __   ☐ ☐ ☐ ☐

_____ __

PM Habits   To Do's

_____ __   _____ __

_____ __   _____ __

_____ __   _____ __

Affirmation:

Saturday _____

AM Habits   Meals

_____ __   B: _____

_____ __   L: _____

_____ __   D:_____

Mid-Day Habits   Water

_____ __   ☐ ☐ ☐ ☐

_____ __   ☐ ☐ ☐ ☐

_____ __

PM Habits   To Do's

_____ __   _____ __

_____ __   _____ __

_____ __   _____ __

Space to Clear Your Mind

Weekly focus:

Sunday _____

AM Habits   Meals
_____ __   B: _____
_____ __   L: _____
_____ __   D:_____

Mid-Day Habits   Water
_____ __   ☐ ☐ ☐ ☐
_____ __   ☐ ☐ ☐ ☐
_____ __

PM Habits   To Do's
_____ __   _____ __
_____ __   _____ __
_____ __   _____ __

Monday _____

AM Habits   Meals
_____ __   B: _____
_____ __   L: _____
_____ __   D:_____

Mid-Day Habits   Water
_____ __   ☐ ☐ ☐ ☐
_____ __   ☐ ☐ ☐ ☐
_____ __

PM Habits   To Do's
_____ __   _____ __
_____ __   _____ __
_____ __   _____ __

Affirmation:

Tuesday _____

AM Habits   Meals
_____ __   B: _____
_____ __   L: _____
_____ __   D:_____

Mid-Day Habits   Water
_____ __   ☐ ☐ ☐ ☐
_____ __   ☐ ☐ ☐ ☐
_____ __

PM Habits   To Do's
_____ __   _____ __
_____ __   _____ __
_____ __   _____ __

Wednesday _____

AM Habits   Meals
_____ __   B: _____
_____ __   L: _____
_____ __   D:_____

Mid-Day Habits   Water
_____ __   ☐ ☐ ☐ ☐
_____ __   ☐ ☐ ☐ ☐
_____ __

PM Habits   To Do's
_____ __   _____ __
_____ __   _____ __
_____ __   _____ __

Monthly intention:

Thursday _____

AM Habits	Meals
_____ __	B: _____
_____ __	L: _____
_____ __	D:_____

Mid-Day Habits	Water
_____ __	☐ ☐ ☐ ☐
_____ __	☐ ☐ ☐ ☐
_____ __	

PM Habits	To Do's
_____ __	_____ __
_____ __	_____ __
_____ __	_____ __

Friday _____

AM Habits	Meals
_____ __	B: _____
_____ __	L: _____
_____ __	D:_____

Mid-Day Habits	Water
_____ __	☐ ☐ ☐ ☐
_____ __	☐ ☐ ☐ ☐
_____ __	

PM Habits	To Do's
_____ __	_____ __
_____ __	_____ __
_____ __	_____ __

Affirmation:

Saturday _____

Space to Clear Your Mind

AM Habits	Meals
_____ __	B: _____
_____ __	L: _____
_____ __	D:_____

Mid-Day Habits	Water
_____ __	☐ ☐ ☐ ☐
_____ __	☐ ☐ ☐ ☐
_____ __	

PM Habits	To Do's
_____ __	_____ __
_____ __	_____ __
_____ __	_____ __

Weekly focus:

Sunday _____

AM Habits | Meals
_____ __ | B: _____
_____ __ | L: _____
_____ __ | D:_____

Mid-Day Habits | Water
_____ __ | ☐ ☐ ☐ ☐
_____ __ | ☐ ☐ ☐ ☐
_____ __ |

PM Habits | To Do's
_____ __ | _____ __
_____ __ | _____ __
_____ __ | _____ __

Monday _____

AM Habits | Meals
_____ __ | B: _____
_____ __ | L: _____
_____ __ | D:_____

Mid-Day Habits | Water
_____ __ | ☐ ☐ ☐ ☐
_____ __ | ☐ ☐ ☐ ☐
_____ __ |

PM Habits | To Do's
_____ __ | _____ __
_____ __ | _____ __
_____ __ | _____ __

Affirmation:

Tuesday _____

AM Habits | Meals
_____ __ | B: _____
_____ __ | L: _____
_____ __ | D:_____

Mid-Day Habits | Water
_____ __ | ☐ ☐ ☐ ☐
_____ __ | ☐ ☐ ☐ ☐
_____ __ |

PM Habits | To Do's
_____ __ | _____ __
_____ __ | _____ __
_____ __ | _____ __

Wednesday _____

AM Habits | Meals
_____ __ | B: _____
_____ __ | L: _____
_____ __ | D:_____

Mid-Day Habits | Water
_____ __ | ☐ ☐ ☐ ☐
_____ __ | ☐ ☐ ☐ ☐
_____ __ |

PM Habits | To Do's
_____ __ | _____ __
_____ __ | _____ __
_____ __ | _____ __

Monthly intention:

Thursday _____

AM Habits
_____ __
_____ __
_____ __

Meals
B: _____
L: _____
D:_____

Mid-Day Habits
_____ __
_____ __
_____ __

Water
☐ ☐ ☐ ☐
☐ ☐ ☐ ☐

PM Habits
_____ __
_____ __
_____ __

To Do's
_____ __
_____ __
_____ __

Friday _____

AM Habits
_____ __
_____ __
_____ __

Meals
B: _____
L: _____
D:_____

Mid-Day Habits
_____ __
_____ __
_____ __

Water
☐ ☐ ☐ ☐
☐ ☐ ☐ ☐

PM Habits
_____ __
_____ __
_____ __

To Do's
_____ __
_____ __
_____ __

Affirmation:

Saturday _____

AM Habits
_____ __
_____ __
_____ __

Meals
B: _____
L: _____
D:_____

Mid-Day Habits
_____ __
_____ __
_____ __

Water
☐ ☐ ☐ ☐
☐ ☐ ☐ ☐

PM Habits
_____ __
_____ __
_____ __

To Do's
_____ __
_____ __
_____ __

Space to Clear Your Mind

Weekly focus:

Sunday _____

AM Habits   Meals
_____ __   B: _____
_____ __   L: _____
_____ __   D: _____

Mid-Day Habits   Water
_____ __   ☐ ☐ ☐ ☐
_____ __   ☐ ☐ ☐ ☐
_____ __

PM Habits   To Do's
_____ __   _____ __
_____ __   _____ __
_____ __   _____ __

Monday _____

AM Habits   Meals
_____ __   B: _____
_____ __   L: _____
_____ __   D: _____

Mid-Day Habits   Water
_____ __   ☐ ☐ ☐ ☐
_____ __   ☐ ☐ ☐ ☐
_____ __

PM Habits   To Do's
_____ __   _____ __
_____ __   _____ __
_____ __   _____ __

Affirmation:

Tuesday _____

AM Habits   Meals
_____ __   B: _____
_____ __   L: _____
_____ __   D: _____

Mid-Day Habits   Water
_____ __   ☐ ☐ ☐ ☐
_____ __   ☐ ☐ ☐ ☐
_____ __

PM Habits   To Do's
_____ __   _____ __
_____ __   _____ __
_____ __   _____ __

Wednesday _____

AM Habits   Meals
_____ __   B: _____
_____ __   L: _____
_____ __   D: _____

Mid-Day Habits   Water
_____ __   ☐ ☐ ☐ ☐
_____ __   ☐ ☐ ☐ ☐
_____ __

PM Habits   To Do's
_____ __   _____ __
_____ __   _____ __
_____ __   _____ __

Monthly intention:

Thursday _____

AM Habits	Meals
_____ __	B: _____
_____ __	L: _____
_____ __	D:_____

Mid-Day Habits   Water

_____ __   ☐ ☐ ☐ ☐
_____ __   ☐ ☐ ☐ ☐
_____ __

PM Habits   To Do's

_____ __   _____ __
_____ __   _____ __
_____ __   _____ __

Friday _____

AM Habits	Meals
_____ __	B: _____
_____ __	L: _____
_____ __	D:_____

Mid-Day Habits   Water

_____ __   ☐ ☐ ☐ ☐
_____ __   ☐ ☐ ☐ ☐
_____ __

PM Habits   To Do's

_____ __   _____ __
_____ __   _____ __
_____ __   _____ __

Affirmation:

Saturday _____

AM Habits	Meals
_____ __	B: _____
_____ __	L: _____
_____ __	D:_____

Mid-Day Habits   Water

_____ __   ☐ ☐ ☐ ☐
_____ __   ☐ ☐ ☐ ☐
_____ __

PM Habits   To Do's

_____ __   _____ __
_____ __   _____ __
_____ __   _____ __

Space to Clear Your Mind

Weekly focus:

Sunday _____   Monday _____

AM Habits   Meals   AM Habits   Meals
_____ __   B: _____   _____ __   B: _____
_____ __   L: _____   _____ __   L: _____
_____ __   D:_____   _____ __   D:_____

Mid-Day Habits   Water   Mid-Day Habits   Water
_____ __   ☐ ☐ ☐ ☐   _____ __   ☐ ☐ ☐ ☐
_____ __   ☐ ☐ ☐ ☐   _____ __   ☐ ☐ ☐ ☐
_____ __

PM Habits   To Do's   PM Habits   To Do's
_____ __   _____ __   _____ __   _____ __
_____ __   _____ __   _____ __   _____ __
_____ __   _____ __   _____ __   _____ __

Affirmation:

Tuesday _____   Wednesday _____

AM Habits   Meals   AM Habits   Meals
_____ __   B: _____   _____ __   B: _____
_____ __   L: _____   _____ __   L: _____
_____ __   D:_____   _____ __   D:_____

Mid-Day Habits   Water   Mid-Day Habits   Water
_____ __   ☐ ☐ ☐ ☐   _____ __   ☐ ☐ ☐ ☐
_____ __   ☐ ☐ ☐ ☐   _____ __   ☐ ☐ ☐ ☐

PM Habits   To Do's   PM Habits   To Do's
_____ __   _____ __   _____ __   _____ __
_____ __   _____ __   _____ __   _____ __
_____ __   _____ __   _____ __   _____ __

♥

Monthly intention:

Thursday _____

AM Habits   Meals
_____ __   B: _____
_____ __   L: _____
_____ __   D:_____

Mid-Day Habits   Water
_____ __   ☐ ☐ ☐ ☐
_____ __   ☐ ☐ ☐ ☐
_____ __

PM Habits   To Do's
_____ __   _____ __
_____ __   _____ __
_____ __   _____ __

Friday _____

AM Habits   Meals
_____ __   B: _____
_____ __   L: _____
_____ __   D:_____

Mid-Day Habits   Water
_____ __   ☐ ☐ ☐ ☐
_____ __   ☐ ☐ ☐ ☐
_____ __

PM Habits   To Do's
_____ __   _____ __
_____ __   _____ __
_____ __   _____ __

Affirmation:

Saturday _____   Space to Clear Your Mind

AM Habits   Meals
_____ __   B: _____
_____ __   L: _____
_____ __   D:_____

Mid-Day Habits   Water
_____ __   ☐ ☐ ☐ ☐
_____ __   ☐ ☐ ☐ ☐
_____ __

PM Habits   To Do's
_____ __   _____ __
_____ __   _____ __
_____ __   _____ __

Weekly focus:

Sunday _____

AM Habits   Meals
_____ __   B: _____
_____ __   L: _____
_____ __   D: _____

Mid-Day Habits   Water
_____ __   ☐ ☐ ☐ ☐
_____ __   ☐ ☐ ☐ ☐
_____ __

PM Habits   To Do's
_____ __   _____ __
_____ __   _____ __
_____ __   _____ __

Monday _____

AM Habits   Meals
_____ __   B: _____
_____ __   L: _____
_____ __   D: _____

Mid-Day Habits   Water
_____ __   ☐ ☐ ☐ ☐
_____ __   ☐ ☐ ☐ ☐
_____ __

PM Habits   To Do's
_____ __   _____ __
_____ __   _____ __
_____ __   _____ __

Affirmation:

Tuesday _____

AM Habits   Meals
_____ __   B: _____
_____ __   L: _____
_____ __   D: _____

Mid-Day Habits   Water
_____ __   ☐ ☐ ☐ ☐
_____ __   ☐ ☐ ☐ ☐
_____ __

PM Habits   To Do's
_____ __   _____ __
_____ __   _____ __
_____ __   _____ __

Wednesday _____

AM Habits   Meals
_____ __   B: _____
_____ __   L: _____
_____ __   D: _____

Mid-Day Habits   Water
_____ __   ☐ ☐ ☐ ☐
_____ __   ☐ ☐ ☐ ☐
_____ __

PM Habits   To Do's
_____ __   _____ __
_____ __   _____ __
_____ __   _____ __

Monthly intention:

Thursday _____

AM Habits   Meals
_____ __   B: _____
_____ __   L: _____
_____ __   D:_____

Mid-Day Habits   Water
_____ __   ☐ ☐ ☐ ☐
_____ __   ☐ ☐ ☐ ☐
_____ __

PM Habits   To Do's
_____ __   _____ __
_____ __   _____ __
_____ __   _____ __

Friday _____

AM Habits   Meals
_____ __   B: _____
_____ __   L: _____
_____ __   D:_____

Mid-Day Habits   Water
_____ __   ☐ ☐ ☐ ☐
_____ __   ☐ ☐ ☐ ☐
_____ __

PM Habits   To Do's
_____ __   _____ __
_____ __   _____ __
_____ __   _____ __

Affirmation:

Saturday _____   Space to Clear Your Mind

AM Habits   Meals
_____ __   B: _____
_____ __   L: _____
_____ __   D:_____

Mid-Day Habits   Water
_____ __   ☐ ☐ ☐ ☐
_____ __   ☐ ☐ ☐ ☐
_____ __

PM Habits   To Do's
_____ __   _____ __
_____ __   _____ __
_____ __   _____ __

♥

Weekly focus:

Sunday _____

AM Habits	Meals
_____ __	B: _____
_____ __	L: _____
_____ __	D:_____

Mid-Day Habits	Water
_____ __	☐ ☐ ☐ ☐
_____ __	☐ ☐ ☐ ☐
_____ __	

PM Habits	To Do's
_____ __	_____ __
_____ __	_____ __
_____ __	_____ __

Monday _____

AM Habits	Meals
_____ __	B: _____
_____ __	L: _____
_____ __	D:_____

Mid-Day Habits	Water
_____ __	☐ ☐ ☐ ☐
_____ __	☐ ☐ ☐ ☐
_____ __	

PM Habits	To Do's
_____ __	_____ __
_____ __	_____ __
_____ __	_____ __

Affirmation:

Tuesday _____

AM Habits	Meals
_____ __	B: _____
_____ __	L: _____
_____ __	D:_____

Mid-Day Habits	Water
_____ __	☐ ☐ ☐ ☐
_____ __	☐ ☐ ☐ ☐
_____ __	

PM Habits	To Do's
_____ __	_____ __
_____ __	_____ __
_____ __	_____ __

Wednesday _____

AM Habits	Meals
_____ __	B: _____
_____ __	L: _____
_____ __	D:_____

Mid-Day Habits	Water
_____ __	☐ ☐ ☐ ☐
_____ __	☐ ☐ ☐ ☐
_____ __	

PM Habits	To Do's
_____ __	_____ __
_____ __	_____ __
_____ __	_____ __

Monthly intention:

Thursday _____

AM Habits	Meals
_____ __	B: _____
_____ __	L: _____
_____ __	D: _____

Mid-Day Habits	Water
_____ __	☐ ☐ ☐ ☐
_____ __	☐ ☐ ☐ ☐
_____ __	

PM Habits	To Do's
_____ __	_____ __
_____ __	_____ __
_____ __	_____ __

Friday _____

AM Habits	Meals
_____ __	B: _____
_____ __	L: _____
_____ __	D: _____

Mid-Day Habits	Water
_____ __	☐ ☐ ☐ ☐
_____ __	☐ ☐ ☐ ☐
_____ __	

PM Habits	To Do's
_____ __	_____ __
_____ __	_____ __
_____ __	_____ __

Affirmation:

Saturday _____

Space to Clear Your Mind

AM Habits	Meals
_____ __	B: _____
_____ __	L: _____
_____ __	D: _____

Mid-Day Habits	Water
_____ __	☐ ☐ ☐ ☐
_____ __	☐ ☐ ☐ ☐
_____ __	

PM Habits	To Do's
_____ __	_____ __
_____ __	_____ __
_____ __	_____ __

Weekly focus:

Sunday _____

AM Habits   Meals
_____ __   B: _____
_____ __   L: _____
_____ __   D:_____

Mid-Day Habits   Water
_____ __   ☐ ☐ ☐ ☐
_____ __   ☐ ☐ ☐ ☐
_____ __

PM Habits   To Do's
_____ __   _____ __
_____ __   _____ __
_____ __   _____ __

Monday _____

AM Habits   Meals
_____ __   B: _____
_____ __   L: _____
_____ __   D:_____

Mid-Day Habits   Water
_____ __   ☐ ☐ ☐ ☐
_____ __   ☐ ☐ ☐ ☐
_____ __

PM Habits   To Do's
_____ __   _____ __
_____ __   _____ __
_____ __   _____ __

Affirmation:

Tuesday _____

AM Habits   Meals
_____ __   B: _____
_____ __   L: _____
_____ __   D:_____

Mid-Day Habits   Water
_____ __   ☐ ☐ ☐ ☐
_____ __   ☐ ☐ ☐ ☐
_____ __

PM Habits   To Do's
_____ __   _____ __
_____ __   _____ __
_____ __   _____ __

Wednesday _____

AM Habits   Meals
_____ __   B: _____
_____ __   L: _____
_____ __   D:_____

Mid-Day Habits   Water
_____ __   ☐ ☐ ☐ ☐
_____ __   ☐ ☐ ☐ ☐
_____ __

PM Habits   To Do's
_____ __   _____ __
_____ __   _____ __
_____ __   _____ __

Monthly intention:

Thursday _____   **Friday** _____

AM Habits	Meals	AM Habits	Meals
_____ __	B: _____	_____ __	B: _____
_____ __	L: _____	_____ __	L: _____
_____ __	D: _____	_____ __	D: _____

Mid-Day Habits	Water	Mid-Day Habits	Water
_____ __	☐ ☐ ☐ ☐	_____ __	☐ ☐ ☐ ☐
_____ __	☐ ☐ ☐ ☐	_____ __	☐ ☐ ☐ ☐

PM Habits	To Do's	PM Habits	To Do's
_____ __	_____ __	_____ __	_____ __
_____ __	_____ __	_____ __	_____ __
_____ __	_____ __	_____ __	_____ __

Affirmation:

Saturday _____   **Space to Clear Your Mind**

AM Habits	Meals
_____ __	B: _____
_____ __	L: _____
_____ __	D: _____

Mid-Day Habits	Water
_____ __	☐ ☐ ☐ ☐
_____ __	☐ ☐ ☐ ☐

PM Habits	To Do's
_____ __	_____ __
_____ __	_____ __
_____ __	_____ __

Weekly focus:

Sunday _____

AM Habits	Meals
_____ __	B: _____
_____ __	L: _____
_____ __	D:_____

Mid-Day Habits	Water
_____ __	☐ ☐ ☐ ☐
_____ __	☐ ☐ ☐ ☐
_____ __	

PM Habits	To Do's
_____ __	_____ __
_____ __	_____ __
_____ __	_____ __

Monday _____

AM Habits	Meals
_____ __	B: _____
_____ __	L: _____
_____ __	D:_____

Mid-Day Habits	Water
_____ __	☐ ☐ ☐ ☐
_____ __	☐ ☐ ☐ ☐
_____ __	

PM Habits	To Do's
_____ __	_____ __
_____ __	_____ __
_____ __	_____ __

Affirmation:

Tuesday _____

AM Habits	Meals
_____ __	B: _____
_____ __	L: _____
_____ __	D:_____

Mid-Day Habits	Water
_____ __	☐ ☐ ☐ ☐
_____ __	☐ ☐ ☐ ☐
_____ __	

PM Habits	To Do's
_____ __	_____ __
_____ __	_____ __
_____ __	_____ __

Wednesday _____

AM Habits	Meals
_____ __	B: _____
_____ __	L: _____
_____ __	D:_____

Mid-Day Habits	Water
_____ __	☐ ☐ ☐ ☐
_____ __	☐ ☐ ☐ ☐
_____ __	

PM Habits	To Do's
_____ __	_____ __
_____ __	_____ __
_____ __	_____ __

Monthly intention:

Thursday _____

AM Habits | Meals
_____ __ | B: _____
_____ __ | L: _____
_____ __ | D:_____

Mid-Day Habits | Water
_____ __ | ☐ ☐ ☐ ☐
_____ __ | ☐ ☐ ☐ ☐
_____ __

PM Habits | To Do's
_____ __ | _____ __
_____ __ | _____ __
_____ __ | _____ __

Friday _____

AM Habits | Meals
_____ __ | B: _____
_____ __ | L: _____
_____ __ | D:_____

Mid-Day Habits | Water
_____ __ | ☐ ☐ ☐ ☐
_____ __ | ☐ ☐ ☐ ☐
_____ __

PM Habits | To Do's
_____ __ | _____ __
_____ __ | _____ __
_____ __ | _____ __

Affirmation:

Saturday _____

Space to Clear Your Mind

AM Habits | Meals
_____ __ | B: _____
_____ __ | L: _____
_____ __ | D:_____

Mid-Day Habits | Water
_____ __ | ☐ ☐ ☐ ☐
_____ __ | ☐ ☐ ☐ ☐
_____ __

PM Habits | To Do's
_____ __ | _____ __
_____ __ | _____ __
_____ __ | _____ __

♥

Weekly focus:

Sunday _____

AM Habits	Meals
_____ __	B: _____
_____ __	L: _____
_____ __	D: _____

Mid-Day Habits	Water
_____ __	☐ ☐ ☐ ☐
_____ __	☐ ☐ ☐ ☐
_____ __	

PM Habits	To Do's
_____ __	_____ __
_____ __	_____ __
_____ __	_____ __

Monday _____

AM Habits	Meals
_____ __	B: _____
_____ __	L: _____
_____ __	D: _____

Mid-Day Habits	Water
_____ __	☐ ☐ ☐ ☐
_____ __	☐ ☐ ☐ ☐
_____ __	

PM Habits	To Do's
_____ __	_____ __
_____ __	_____ __
_____ __	_____ __

Affirmation:

Tuesday _____

AM Habits	Meals
_____ __	B: _____
_____ __	L: _____
_____ __	D: _____

Mid-Day Habits	Water
_____ __	☐ ☐ ☐ ☐
_____ __	☐ ☐ ☐ ☐
_____ __	

PM Habits	To Do's
_____ __	_____ __
_____ __	_____ __
_____ __	_____ __

Wednesday _____

AM Habits	Meals
_____ __	B: _____
_____ __	L: _____
_____ __	D: _____

Mid-Day Habits	Water
_____ __	☐ ☐ ☐ ☐
_____ __	☐ ☐ ☐ ☐
_____ __	

PM Habits	To Do's
_____ __	_____ __
_____ __	_____ __
_____ __	_____ __

Monthly intention:

Thursday _____

AM Habits   Meals
_____ __   B: _____
_____ __   L: _____
_____ __   D:_____

Mid-Day Habits   Water
_____ __   ☐ ☐ ☐ ☐
_____ __   ☐ ☐ ☐ ☐

PM Habits   To Do's
_____ __   _____ __
_____ __   _____ __
_____ __   _____ __

Friday _____

AM Habits   Meals
_____ __   B: _____
_____ __   L: _____
_____ __   D:_____

Mid-Day Habits   Water
_____ __   ☐ ☐ ☐ ☐
_____ __   ☐ ☐ ☐ ☐

PM Habits   To Do's
_____ __   _____ __
_____ __   _____ __
_____ __   _____ __

Affirmation:

Saturday _____   Space to Clear Your Mind

AM Habits   Meals
_____ __   B: _____
_____ __   L: _____
_____ __   D:_____

Mid-Day Habits   Water
_____ __   ☐ ☐ ☐ ☐
_____ __   ☐ ☐ ☐ ☐

PM Habits   To Do's
_____ __   _____ __
_____ __   _____ __
_____ __   _____ __

Weekly focus:

Sunday _____

AM Habits   Meals
_____ __   B: _____
_____ __   L: _____
_____ __   D: _____

Mid-Day Habits   Water
_____ __   ☐ ☐ ☐ ☐
_____ __   ☐ ☐ ☐ ☐
_____ __

PM Habits   To Do's
_____ __   _____ __
_____ __   _____ __
_____ __   _____ __

Monday _____

AM Habits   Meals
_____ __   B: _____
_____ __   L: _____
_____ __   D: _____

Mid-Day Habits   Water
_____ __   ☐ ☐ ☐ ☐
_____ __   ☐ ☐ ☐ ☐
_____ __

PM Habits   To Do's
_____ __   _____ __
_____ __   _____ __
_____ __   _____ __

Affirmation:

Tuesday _____

AM Habits   Meals
_____ __   B: _____
_____ __   L: _____
_____ __   D: _____

Mid-Day Habits   Water
_____ __   ☐ ☐ ☐ ☐
_____ __   ☐ ☐ ☐ ☐
_____ __

PM Habits   To Do's
_____ __   _____ __
_____ __   _____ __
_____ __   _____ __

Wednesday _____

AM Habits   Meals
_____ __   B: _____
_____ __   L: _____
_____ __   D: _____

Mid-Day Habits   Water
_____ __   ☐ ☐ ☐ ☐
_____ __   ☐ ☐ ☐ ☐
_____ __

PM Habits   To Do's
_____ __   _____ __
_____ __   _____ __
_____ __   _____ __

Monthly intention:

Thursday _____

AM Habits | Meals
_____ __ | B: _____
_____ __ | L: _____
_____ __ | D:_____

Mid-Day Habits | Water
_____ __ | ☐ ☐ ☐ ☐
_____ __ | ☐ ☐ ☐ ☐
_____ __ |

PM Habits | To Do's
_____ __ | _____ __
_____ __ | _____ __
_____ __ | _____ __

Friday _____

AM Habits | Meals
_____ __ | B: _____
_____ __ | L: _____
_____ __ | D:_____

Mid-Day Habits | Water
_____ __ | ☐ ☐ ☐ ☐
_____ __ | ☐ ☐ ☐ ☐
_____ __ |

PM Habits | To Do's
_____ __ | _____ __
_____ __ | _____ __
_____ __ | _____ __

Affirmation:

Saturday _____

AM Habits | Meals
_____ __ | B: _____
_____ __ | L: _____
_____ __ | D:_____

Mid-Day Habits | Water
_____ __ | ☐ ☐ ☐ ☐
_____ __ | ☐ ☐ ☐ ☐
_____ __ |

PM Habits | To Do's
_____ __ | _____ __
_____ __ | _____ __
_____ __ | _____ __

Space to Clear Your Mind

♥

Weekly focus:

Sunday _____

AM Habits   Meals
_____ __   B: _____
_____ __   L: _____
_____ __   D:_____

Mid-Day Habits   Water
_____ __   ☐ ☐ ☐ ☐
_____ __   ☐ ☐ ☐ ☐
_____ __

PM Habits   To Do's
_____ __   _____ __
_____ __   _____ __
_____ __   _____ __

Monday _____

AM Habits   Meals
_____ __   B: _____
_____ __   L: _____
_____ __   D:_____

Mid-Day Habits   Water
_____ __   ☐ ☐ ☐ ☐
_____ __   ☐ ☐ ☐ ☐
_____ __

PM Habits   To Do's
_____ __   _____ __
_____ __   _____ __
_____ __   _____ __

Affirmation:

Tuesday _____

AM Habits   Meals
_____ __   B: _____
_____ __   L: _____
_____ __   D:_____

Mid-Day Habits   Water
_____ __   ☐ ☐ ☐ ☐
_____ __   ☐ ☐ ☐ ☐
_____ __

PM Habits   To Do's
_____ __   _____ __
_____ __   _____ __
_____ __   _____ __

Wednesday _____

AM Habits   Meals
_____ __   B: _____
_____ __   L: _____
_____ __   D:_____

Mid-Day Habits   Water
_____ __   ☐ ☐ ☐ ☐
_____ __   ☐ ☐ ☐ ☐
_____ __

PM Habits   To Do's
_____ __   _____ __
_____ __   _____ __
_____ __   _____ __

♥

Monthly intention:

Thursday _____

AM Habits   Meals
_____ __   B: _____
_____ __   L: _____
_____ __   D:_____

Mid-Day Habits   Water
_____ __   ☐ ☐ ☐ ☐
_____ __   ☐ ☐ ☐ ☐
_____ __

PM Habits   To Do's
_____ __   _____ __
_____ __   _____ __
_____ __   _____ __

Friday _____

AM Habits   Meals
_____ __   B: _____
_____ __   L: _____
_____ __   D:_____

Mid-Day Habits   Water
_____ __   ☐ ☐ ☐ ☐
_____ __   ☐ ☐ ☐ ☐
_____ __

PM Habits   To Do's
_____ __   _____ __
_____ __   _____ __
_____ __   _____ __

Affirmation:

Saturday _____   Space to Clear Your Mind

AM Habits   Meals
_____ __   B: _____
_____ __   L: _____
_____ __   D:_____

Mid-Day Habits   Water
_____ __   ☐ ☐ ☐ ☐
_____ __   ☐ ☐ ☐ ☐
_____ __

PM Habits   To Do's
_____ __   _____ __
_____ __   _____ __
_____ __   _____ __

Weekly focus:

Sunday _____

AM Habits
_____ __
_____ __
_____ __

Meals
B: _____
L: _____
D: _____

Mid-Day Habits
_____ __
_____ __
_____ __

Water
☐ ☐ ☐ ☐
☐ ☐ ☐ ☐

PM Habits
_____ __
_____ __
_____ __

To Do's
_____ __
_____ __
_____ __

Monday _____

AM Habits
_____ __
_____ __
_____ __

Meals
B: _____
L: _____
D: _____

Mid-Day Habits
_____ __
_____ __
_____ __

Water
☐ ☐ ☐ ☐
☐ ☐ ☐ ☐

PM Habits
_____ __
_____ __
_____ __

To Do's
_____ __
_____ __
_____ __

Affirmation:

Tuesday _____

AM Habits
_____ __
_____ __
_____ __

Meals
B: _____
L: _____
D: _____

Mid-Day Habits
_____ __
_____ __

Water
☐ ☐ ☐ ☐
☐ ☐ ☐ ☐

PM Habits
_____ __
_____ __
_____ __

To Do's
_____ __
_____ __
_____ __

Wednesday _____

AM Habits
_____ __
_____ __
_____ __

Meals
B: _____
L: _____
D: _____

Mid-Day Habits
_____ __
_____ __

Water
☐ ☐ ☐ ☐
☐ ☐ ☐ ☐

PM Habits
_____ __
_____ __
_____ __

To Do's
_____ __
_____ __
_____ __

Monthly intention:

Thursday _____

AM Habits | Meals
_____ __ | B: _____
_____ __ | L: _____
_____ __ | D:_____

Mid-Day Habits | Water
_____ __ | ☐ ☐ ☐ ☐
_____ __ | ☐ ☐ ☐ ☐
_____ __ |

PM Habits | To Do's
_____ __ | _____ __
_____ __ | _____ __
_____ __ | _____ __

Friday _____

AM Habits | Meals
_____ __ | B: _____
_____ __ | L: _____
_____ __ | D:_____

Mid-Day Habits | Water
_____ __ | ☐ ☐ ☐ ☐
_____ __ | ☐ ☐ ☐ ☐
_____ __ |

PM Habits | To Do's
_____ __ | _____ __
_____ __ | _____ __
_____ __ | _____ __

Affirmation:

Saturday _____

AM Habits | Meals
_____ __ | B: _____
_____ __ | L: _____
_____ __ | D:_____

Mid-Day Habits | Water
_____ __ | ☐ ☐ ☐ ☐
_____ __ | ☐ ☐ ☐ ☐
_____ __ |

PM Habits | To Do's
_____ __ | _____ __
_____ __ | _____ __
_____ __ | _____ __

Space to Clear Your Mind

Weekly focus:

Sunday _____

AM Habits
_____ __
_____ __
_____ __

Meals
B: _____
L: _____
D:_____

Mid-Day Habits
_____ __
_____ __
_____ __

Water
☐ ☐ ☐ ☐
☐ ☐ ☐ ☐

PM Habits
_____ __
_____ __
_____ __

To Do's
_____ __
_____ __
_____ __

Monday _____

AM Habits
_____ __
_____ __
_____ __

Meals
B: _____
L: _____
D:_____

Mid-Day Habits
_____ __
_____ __
_____ __

Water
☐ ☐ ☐ ☐
☐ ☐ ☐ ☐

PM Habits
_____ __
_____ __
_____ __

To Do's
_____ __
_____ __
_____ __

Affirmation:

Tuesday _____

AM Habits
_____ __
_____ __
_____ __

Meals
B: _____
L: _____
D:_____

Mid-Day Habits
_____ __
_____ __
_____ __

Water
☐ ☐ ☐ ☐
☐ ☐ ☐ ☐

PM Habits
_____ __
_____ __
_____ __

To Do's
_____ __
_____ __
_____ __

Wednesday _____

AM Habits
_____ __
_____ __
_____ __

Meals
B: _____
L: _____
D:_____

Mid-Day Habits
_____ __
_____ __
_____ __

Water
☐ ☐ ☐ ☐
☐ ☐ ☐ ☐

PM Habits
_____ __
_____ __
_____ __

To Do's
_____ __
_____ __
_____ __

♥

Monthly intention:

Thursday _____

AM Habits   Meals
_____ __   B: _____
_____ __   L: _____
_____ __   D:_____

Mid-Day Habits   Water
_____ __   ☐ ☐ ☐ ☐
_____ __   ☐ ☐ ☐ ☐
_____ __

PM Habits   To Do's
_____ __   _____ __
_____ __   _____ __
_____ __   _____ __

Friday _____

AM Habits   Meals
_____ __   B: _____
_____ __   L: _____
_____ __   D:_____

Mid-Day Habits   Water
_____ __   ☐ ☐ ☐ ☐
_____ __   ☐ ☐ ☐ ☐
_____ __

PM Habits   To Do's
_____ __   _____ __
_____ __   _____ __
_____ __   _____ __

Affirmation:

Saturday _____

AM Habits   Meals
_____ __   B: _____
_____ __   L: _____
_____ __   D:_____

Mid-Day Habits   Water
_____ __   ☐ ☐ ☐ ☐
_____ __   ☐ ☐ ☐ ☐
_____ __

PM Habits   To Do's
_____ __   _____ __
_____ __   _____ __
_____ __   _____ __

Space to Clear Your Mind

Weekly focus:

Sunday _____

AM Habits	Meals
_____ __	B: _____
_____ __	L: _____
_____ __	D:_____

Mid-Day Habits	Water
_____ __	☐ ☐ ☐ ☐
_____ __	☐ ☐ ☐ ☐
_____ __	

PM Habits	To Do's
_____ __	_____ __
_____ __	_____ __
_____ __	_____ __

Monday _____

AM Habits	Meals
_____ __	B: _____
_____ __	L: _____
_____ __	D:_____

Mid-Day Habits	Water
_____ __	☐ ☐ ☐ ☐
_____ __	☐ ☐ ☐ ☐
_____ __	

PM Habits	To Do's
_____ __	_____ __
_____ __	_____ __
_____ __	_____ __

Affirmation:

Tuesday _____

AM Habits	Meals
_____ __	B: _____
_____ __	L: _____
_____ __	D:_____

Mid-Day Habits	Water
_____ __	☐ ☐ ☐ ☐
_____ __	☐ ☐ ☐ ☐
_____ __	

PM Habits	To Do's
_____ __	_____ __
_____ __	_____ __
_____ __	_____ __

Wednesday _____

AM Habits	Meals
_____ __	B: _____
_____ __	L: _____
_____ __	D:_____

Mid-Day Habits	Water
_____ __	☐ ☐ ☐ ☐
_____ __	☐ ☐ ☐ ☐
_____ __	

PM Habits	To Do's
_____ __	_____ __
_____ __	_____ __
_____ __	_____ __

Monthly intention:

Thursday _____

AM Habits | Meals
_____ __ | B: _____
_____ __ | L: _____
_____ __ | D:_____

Mid-Day Habits | Water
_____ __ | ☐ ☐ ☐ ☐
_____ __ | ☐ ☐ ☐ ☐
_____ __ |

PM Habits | To Do's
_____ __ | _____ __
_____ __ | _____ __
_____ __ | _____ __

Friday _____

AM Habits | Meals
_____ __ | B: _____
_____ __ | L: _____
_____ __ | D:_____

Mid-Day Habits | Water
_____ __ | ☐ ☐ ☐ ☐
_____ __ | ☐ ☐ ☐ ☐
_____ __ |

PM Habits | To Do's
_____ __ | _____ __
_____ __ | _____ __
_____ __ | _____ __

Affirmation:

Saturday _____

Space to Clear Your Mind

AM Habits | Meals
_____ __ | B: _____
_____ __ | L: _____
_____ __ | D:_____

Mid-Day Habits | Water
_____ __ | ☐ ☐ ☐ ☐
_____ __ | ☐ ☐ ☐ ☐
_____ __ |

PM Habits | To Do's
_____ __ | _____ __
_____ __ | _____ __
_____ __ | _____ __

Weekly focus:

Sunday _____

AM Habits | Meals
_____ __ | B: _____
_____ __ | L: _____
_____ __ | D:_____

Mid-Day Habits | Water
_____ __ | ☐ ☐ ☐ ☐
_____ __ | ☐ ☐ ☐ ☐

PM Habits | To Do's
_____ __ | _____ __
_____ __ | _____ __
_____ __ | _____ __

Monday _____

AM Habits | Meals
_____ __ | B: _____
_____ __ | L: _____
_____ __ | D:_____

Mid-Day Habits | Water
_____ __ | ☐ ☐ ☐ ☐
_____ __ | ☐ ☐ ☐ ☐

PM Habits | To Do's
_____ __ | _____ __
_____ __ | _____ __
_____ __ | _____ __

Affirmation:

Tuesday _____

AM Habits | Meals
_____ __ | B: _____
_____ __ | L: _____
_____ __ | D:_____

Mid-Day Habits | Water
_____ __ | ☐ ☐ ☐ ☐
_____ __ | ☐ ☐ ☐ ☐

PM Habits | To Do's
_____ __ | _____ __
_____ __ | _____ __
_____ __ | _____ __

Wednesday _____

AM Habits | Meals
_____ __ | B: _____
_____ __ | L: _____
_____ __ | D:_____

Mid-Day Habits | Water
_____ __ | ☐ ☐ ☐ ☐
_____ __ | ☐ ☐ ☐ ☐

PM Habits | To Do's
_____ __ | _____ __
_____ __ | _____ __
_____ __ | _____ __

Monthly intention:

Thursday _____

AM Habits   Meals
_____ __   B: _____
_____ __   L: _____
_____ __   D: _____

Mid-Day Habits   Water
_____ __   ☐ ☐ ☐ ☐
_____ __   ☐ ☐ ☐ ☐
_____ __

PM Habits   To Do's
_____ __   _____ __
_____ __   _____ __
_____ __   _____ __

Friday _____

AM Habits   Meals
_____ __   B: _____
_____ __   L: _____
_____ __   D: _____

Mid-Day Habits   Water
_____ __   ☐ ☐ ☐ ☐
_____ __   ☐ ☐ ☐ ☐
_____ __

PM Habits   To Do's
_____ __   _____ __
_____ __   _____ __
_____ __   _____ __

Affirmation:

Saturday _____   Space to Clear Your Mind

AM Habits   Meals
_____ __   B: _____
_____ __   L: _____
_____ __   D: _____

Mid-Day Habits   Water
_____ __   ☐ ☐ ☐ ☐
_____ __   ☐ ☐ ☐ ☐
_____ __

PM Habits   To Do's
_____ __   _____ __
_____ __   _____ __
_____ __   _____ __

Weekly focus:

Sunday _____

AM Habits   Meals
_____ __   B: _____
_____ __   L: _____
_____ __   D:_____

Mid-Day Habits   Water
_____ __   ☐ ☐ ☐ ☐
_____ __   ☐ ☐ ☐ ☐
_____ __

PM Habits   To Do's
_____ __   _____ __
_____ __   _____ __
_____ __   _____ __

Monday _____

AM Habits   Meals
_____ __   B: _____
_____ __   L: _____
_____ __   D:_____

Mid-Day Habits   Water
_____ __   ☐ ☐ ☐ ☐
_____ __   ☐ ☐ ☐ ☐
_____ _

PM Habits   To Do's
_____ __   _____ __
_____ __   _____ __
_____ __   _____ __

Affirmation:

Tuesday _____

AM Habits   Meals
_____ __   B: _____
_____ __   L: _____
_____ __   D:_____

Mid-Day Habits   Water
_____ __   ☐ ☐ ☐ ☐
_____ __   ☐ ☐ ☐ ☐
_____ __

PM Habits   To Do's
_____ __   _____ __
_____ __   _____ __
_____ __   _____ __

Wednesday _____

AM Habits   Meals
_____ __   B: _____
_____ __   L: _____
_____ __   D:_____

Mid-Day Habits   Water
_____ __   ☐ ☐ ☐ ☐
_____ __   ☐ ☐ ☐ ☐
_____ _

PM Habits   To Do's
_____ __   _____ __
_____ __   _____ __
_____ __   _____ __

Monthly intention:

Thursday _____

AM Habits
_____ __
_____ __
_____ __

Meals
B: _____
L: _____
D:_____

Mid-Day Habits
_____ __
_____ __
_____ __

Water
☐ ☐ ☐ ☐
☐ ☐ ☐ ☐

PM Habits
_____ __
_____ __
_____ __

To Do's
_____ __
_____ __
_____ __

Friday _____

AM Habits
_____ __
_____ __
_____ __

Meals
B: _____
L: _____
D:_____

Mid-Day Habits
_____ __
_____ __
_____ __

Water
☐ ☐ ☐ ☐
☐ ☐ ☐ ☐

PM Habits
_____ __
_____ __
_____ __

To Do's
_____ __
_____ __
_____ __

Affirmation:

Saturday _____

Space to Clear Your Mind

AM Habits
_____ __
_____ __
_____ __

Meals
B: _____
L: _____
D:_____

Mid-Day Habits
_____ __
_____ __
_____ __

Water
☐ ☐ ☐ ☐
☐ ☐ ☐ ☐

PM Habits
_____ __
_____ __
_____ __

To Do's
_____ __
_____ __
_____ __

Weekly focus:

Sunday _____

AM Habits   Meals
_____ __   B: _____
_____ __   L: _____
_____ __   D:_____

Mid-Day Habits   Water
_____ __   ☐ ☐ ☐ ☐
_____ __   ☐ ☐ ☐ ☐
_____ __

PM Habits   To Do's
_____ __   _____ __
_____ __   _____ __
_____ __   _____ __

Monday _____

AM Habits   Meals
_____ __   B: _____
_____ __   L: _____
_____ __   D:_____

Mid-Day Habits   Water
_____ __   ☐ ☐ ☐ ☐
_____ __   ☐ ☐ ☐ ☐
_____ __

PM Habits   To Do's
_____ __   _____ __
_____ __   _____ __
_____ __   _____ __

Affirmation:

Tuesday _____

AM Habits   Meals
_____ __   B: _____
_____ __   L: _____
_____ __   D:_____

Mid-Day Habits   Water
_____ __   ☐ ☐ ☐ ☐
_____ __   ☐ ☐ ☐ ☐
_____ __

PM Habits   To Do's
_____ __   _____ __
_____ __   _____ __
_____ __   _____ __

Wednesday _____

AM Habits   Meals
_____ __   B: _____
_____ __   L: _____
_____ __   D:_____

Mid-Day Habits   Water
_____ __   ☐ ☐ ☐ ☐
_____ __   ☐ ☐ ☐ ☐
_____ __

PM Habits   To Do's
_____ __   _____ __
_____ __   _____ __
_____ __   _____ __

Monthly intention:

Thursday _____

AM Habits   Meals
_____ __   B: _____
_____ __   L: _____
_____ __   D: _____

Mid-Day Habits   Water
_____ __   ☐ ☐ ☐ ☐
_____ __   ☐ ☐ ☐ ☐
_____ __

PM Habits   To Do's
_____ __   _____ __
_____ __   _____ __
_____ __   _____ __

Friday _____

AM Habits   Meals
_____ __   B: _____
_____ __   L: _____
_____ __   D: _____

Mid-Day Habits   Water
_____ __   ☐ ☐ ☐ ☐
_____ __   ☐ ☐ ☐ ☐
_____ __

PM Habits   To Do's
_____ __   _____ __
_____ __   _____ __
_____ __   _____ __

Affirmation:

Saturday _____

AM Habits   Meals
_____ __   B: _____
_____ __   L: _____
_____ __   D: _____

Mid-Day Habits   Water
_____ __   ☐ ☐ ☐ ☐
_____ __   ☐ ☐ ☐ ☐
_____ __

PM Habits   To Do's
_____ __   _____ __
_____ __   _____ __
_____ __   _____ __

Space to Clear Your Mind

Weekly focus:

Sunday _____

AM Habits	Meals
_____ __	B: _____
_____ __	L: _____
_____ __	D:_____

Mid-Day Habits	Water
_____ __	☐ ☐ ☐ ☐
_____ __	☐ ☐ ☐ ☐
_____ __	

PM Habits	To Do's
_____ __	_____ __
_____ __	_____ __
_____ __	_____ __

Monday _____

AM Habits	Meals
_____ __	B: _____
_____ __	L: _____
_____ __	D:_____

Mid-Day Habits	Water
_____ __	☐ ☐ ☐ ☐
_____ __	☐ ☐ ☐ ☐
_____ __	

PM Habits	To Do's
_____ __	_____ __
_____ __	_____ __
_____ __	_____ __

Affirmation:

Tuesday _____

AM Habits	Meals
_____ __	B: _____
_____ __	L: _____
_____ __	D:_____

Mid-Day Habits	Water
_____ __	☐ ☐ ☐ ☐
_____ __	☐ ☐ ☐ ☐
_____ __	

PM Habits	To Do's
_____ __	_____ __
_____ __	_____ __
_____ __	_____ __

Wednesday _____

AM Habits	Meals
_____ __	B: _____
_____ __	L: _____
_____ __	D:_____

Mid-Day Habits	Water
_____ __	☐ ☐ ☐ ☐
_____ __	☐ ☐ ☐ ☐
_____ __	

PM Habits	To Do's
_____ __	_____ __
_____ __	_____ __
_____ __	_____ __

Monthly intention:

Thursday _____

AM Habits   Meals
_____ __   B: _____
_____ __   L: _____
_____ __   D: _____

Mid-Day Habits   Water
_____ __   ☐ ☐ ☐ ☐
_____ __   ☐ ☐ ☐ ☐
_____ __

PM Habits   To Do's
_____ __   _____ __
_____ __   _____ __
_____ __   _____ __

Friday _____

AM Habits   Meals
_____ __   B: _____
_____ __   L: _____
_____ __   D: _____

Mid-Day Habits   Water
_____ __   ☐ ☐ ☐ ☐
_____ __   ☐ ☐ ☐ ☐
_____ __

PM Habits   To Do's
_____ __   _____ __
_____ __   _____ __
_____ __   _____ __

Affirmation:

Saturday _____

AM Habits   Meals
_____ __   B: _____
_____ __   L: _____
_____ __   D: _____

Mid-Day Habits   Water
_____ __   ☐ ☐ ☐ ☐
_____ __   ☐ ☐ ☐ ☐
_____ __

PM Habits   To Do's
_____ __   _____ __
_____ __   _____ __
_____ __   _____ __

Space to Clear Your Mind

Weekly focus:

Sunday _____

AM Habits   Meals
_____ __   B: _____
_____ __   L: _____
_____ __   D:_____

Mid-Day Habits   Water
_____ __   ☐ ☐ ☐ ☐
_____ __   ☐ ☐ ☐ ☐

PM Habits   To Do's
_____ __   _____ __
_____ __   _____ __
_____ __   _____ __

Monday _____

AM Habits   Meals
_____ __   B: _____
_____ __   L: _____
_____ __   D:_____

Mid-Day Habits   Water
_____ __   ☐ ☐ ☐ ☐
_____ __   ☐ ☐ ☐ ☐

PM Habits   To Do's
_____ __   _____ __
_____ __   _____ __
_____ __   _____ __

Affirmation:

Tuesday _____

AM Habits   Meals
_____ __   B: _____
_____ __   L: _____
_____ __   D:_____

Mid-Day Habits   Water
_____ __   ☐ ☐ ☐ ☐
_____ __   ☐ ☐ ☐ ☐

PM Habits   To Do's
_____ __   _____ __
_____ __   _____ __
_____ __   _____ __

Wednesday _____

AM Habits   Meals
_____ __   B: _____
_____ __   L: _____
_____ __   D:_____

Mid-Day Habits   Water
_____ __   ☐ ☐ ☐ ☐
_____ __   ☐ ☐ ☐ ☐

PM Habits   To Do's
_____ __   _____ __
_____ __   _____ __
_____ __   _____ __

Monthly intention:

Thursday _____

AM Habits   Meals
_____ __   B: _____
_____ __   L: _____
_____ __   D:_____

Mid-Day Habits   Water
_____ __   ☐ ☐ ☐ ☐
_____ __   ☐ ☐ ☐ ☐
_____ __

PM Habits   To Do's
_____ __   _____ __
_____ __   _____ __
_____ __   _____ __

Friday _____

AM Habits   Meals
_____ __   B: _____
_____ __   L: _____
_____ __   D:_____

Mid-Day Habits   Water
_____ __   ☐ ☐ ☐ ☐
_____ __   ☐ ☐ ☐ ☐
_____ __

PM Habits   To Do's
_____ __   _____ __
_____ __   _____ __
_____ __   _____ __

Affirmation:

Saturday _____

AM Habits   Meals
_____ __   B: _____
_____ __   L: _____
_____ __   D:_____

Mid-Day Habits   Water
_____ __   ☐ ☐ ☐ ☐
_____ __   ☐ ☐ ☐ ☐
_____ __

PM Habits   To Do's
_____ __   _____ __
_____ __   _____ __
_____ __   _____ __

Space to Clear Your Mind

Weekly focus:

Sunday _____

AM Habits | Meals
_____ __ | B: _____
_____ __ | L: _____
_____ __ | D: _____

Mid-Day Habits | Water
_____ __ | ☐ ☐ ☐ ☐
_____ __ | ☐ ☐ ☐ ☐
_____ __

PM Habits | To Do's
_____ __ | _____ __
_____ __ | _____ __
_____ __ | _____ __

Monday _____

AM Habits | Meals
_____ __ | B: _____
_____ __ | L: _____
_____ __ | D: _____

Mid-Day Habits | Water
_____ __ | ☐ ☐ ☐ ☐
_____ __ | ☐ ☐ ☐ ☐
_____ __

PM Habits | To Do's
_____ __ | _____ __
_____ __ | _____ __
_____ __ | _____ __

Affirmation:

Tuesday _____

AM Habits | Meals
_____ __ | B: _____
_____ __ | L: _____
_____ __ | D: _____

Mid-Day Habits | Water
_____ __ | ☐ ☐ ☐ ☐
_____ __ | ☐ ☐ ☐ ☐
_____ __

PM Habits | To Do's
_____ __ | _____ __
_____ __ | _____ __
_____ __ | _____ __

Wednesday _____

AM Habits | Meals
_____ __ | B: _____
_____ __ | L: _____
_____ __ | D: _____

Mid-Day Habits | Water
_____ __ | ☐ ☐ ☐ ☐
_____ __ | ☐ ☐ ☐ ☐
_____ __

PM Habits | To Do's
_____ __ | _____ __
_____ __ | _____ __
_____ __ | _____ __

Monthly intention:

Thursday _____   Friday _____

AM Habits   Meals   AM Habits   Meals
_____ __   B: _____   _____ __   B: _____
_____ __   L: _____   _____ __   L: _____
_____ __   D:_____   _____ __   D:_____

Mid-Day Habits   Water   Mid-Day Habits   Water
_____ __   ☐ ☐ ☐ ☐   _____ __   ☐ ☐ ☐ ☐
_____ __   ☐ ☐ ☐ ☐   _____ __   ☐ ☐ ☐ ☐
_____ __   _____ __

PM Habits   To Do's   PM Habits   To Do's
_____ __   _____ __   _____ __   _____ __
_____ __   _____ __   _____ __   _____ __
_____ __   _____ __   _____ __   _____ __

Affirmation:

Saturday _____   Space to Clear Your Mind

AM Habits   Meals
_____ __   B: _____
_____ __   L: _____
_____ __   D:_____

Mid-Day Habits   Water
_____ __   ☐ ☐ ☐ ☐
_____ __   ☐ ☐ ☐ ☐
_____ __

PM Habits   To Do's
_____ __   _____ __
_____ __   _____ __
_____ __   _____ __

♥

Weekly focus:

Sunday _____

AM Habits	Meals
_____ __	B: _____
_____ __	L: _____
_____ __	D: _____

Mid-Day Habits	Water
_____ __	☐ ☐ ☐ ☐
_____ __	☐ ☐ ☐ ☐
_____ __	

PM Habits	To Do's
_____ __	_____ __
_____ __	_____ __
_____ __	_____ __

Monday _____

AM Habits	Meals
_____ __	B: _____
_____ __	L: _____
_____ __	D: _____

Mid-Day Habits	Water
_____ __	☐ ☐ ☐ ☐
_____ __	☐ ☐ ☐ ☐
_____ __	

PM Habits	To Do's
_____ __	_____ __
_____ __	_____ __
_____ __	_____ __

Affirmation:

Tuesday _____

AM Habits	Meals
_____ __	B: _____
_____ __	L: _____
_____ __	D: _____

Mid-Day Habits	Water
_____ __	☐ ☐ ☐ ☐
_____ __	☐ ☐ ☐ ☐
_____ __	

PM Habits	To Do's
_____ __	_____ __
_____ __	_____ __
_____ __	_____ __

Wednesday _____

AM Habits	Meals
_____ __	B: _____
_____ __	L: _____
_____ __	D: _____

Mid-Day Habits	Water
_____ __	☐ ☐ ☐ ☐
_____ __	☐ ☐ ☐ ☐
_____ __	

PM Habits	To Do's
_____ __	_____ __
_____ __	_____ __
_____ __	_____ __

Monthly intention:

Thursday _____

AM Habits   Meals
_____ __   B: _____
_____ __   L: _____
_____ __   D:_____

Mid-Day Habits   Water
_____ __   ☐ ☐ ☐ ☐
_____ __   ☐ ☐ ☐ ☐

PM Habits   To Do's
_____ __   _____ __
_____ __   _____ __
_____ __   _____ __

Friday _____

AM Habits   Meals
_____ __   B: _____
_____ __   L: _____
_____ __   D:_____

Mid-Day Habits   Water
_____ __   ☐ ☐ ☐ ☐
_____ __   ☐ ☐ ☐ ☐

PM Habits   To Do's
_____ __   _____ __
_____ __   _____ __
_____ __   _____ __

Affirmation:

Saturday _____

AM Habits   Meals
_____ __   B: _____
_____ __   L: _____
_____ __   D:_____

Mid-Day Habits   Water
_____ __   ☐ ☐ ☐ ☐
_____ __   ☐ ☐ ☐ ☐

PM Habits   To Do's
_____ __   _____ __
_____ __   _____ __
_____ __   _____ __

Space to Clear Your Mind

Weekly focus:

Sunday _____

AM Habits	Meals
_____ __	B: _____
_____ __	L: _____
_____ __	D: _____

Mid-Day Habits   Water

☐ ☐ ☐ ☐
☐ ☐ ☐ ☐

PM Habits   To Do's

Monday _____

AM Habits	Meals
_____ __	B: _____
_____ __	L: _____
_____ __	D: _____

Mid-Day Habits   Water

☐ ☐ ☐ ☐
☐ ☐ ☐ ☐

PM Habits   To Do's

Affirmation:

Tuesday _____

AM Habits	Meals
_____ __	B: _____
_____ __	L: _____
_____ __	D: _____

Mid-Day Habits   Water

☐ ☐ ☐ ☐
☐ ☐ ☐ ☐

PM Habits   To Do's

Wednesday _____

AM Habits	Meals
_____ __	B: _____
_____ __	L: _____
_____ __	D: _____

Mid-Day Habits   Water

☐ ☐ ☐ ☐
☐ ☐ ☐ ☐

PM Habits   To Do's

Monthly intention:

Thursday _____

AM Habits   Meals
_____ __   B: _____
_____ __   L: _____
_____ __   D: _____

Mid-Day Habits   Water
_____ __   ☐ ☐ ☐ ☐
_____ __   ☐ ☐ ☐ ☐
_____ __

PM Habits   To Do's
_____ __   _____ __
_____ __   _____ __
_____ __   _____ __

Friday _____

AM Habits   Meals
_____ __   B: _____
_____ __   L: _____
_____ __   D: _____

Mid-Day Habits   Water
_____ __   ☐ ☐ ☐ ☐
_____ __   ☐ ☐ ☐ ☐
_____ __

PM Habits   To Do's
_____ __   _____ __
_____ __   _____ __
_____ __   _____ __

Affirmation:

Saturday _____

AM Habits   Meals
_____ __   B: _____
_____ __   L: _____
_____ __   D: _____

Mid-Day Habits   Water
_____ __   ☐ ☐ ☐ ☐
_____ __   ☐ ☐ ☐ ☐
_____ __

PM Habits   To Do's
_____ __   _____ __
_____ __   _____ __
_____ __   _____ __

Space to Clear Your Mind

Weekly focus:

Sunday _____

AM Habits | Meals
_____ __ | B: _____
_____ __ | L: _____
_____ __ | D: _____

Mid-Day Habits | Water
_____ __ | ☐ ☐ ☐ ☐
_____ __ | ☐ ☐ ☐ ☐
_____ __ |

PM Habits | To Do's
_____ __ | _____ __
_____ __ | _____ __
_____ __ | _____ __

Monday _____

AM Habits | Meals
_____ __ | B: _____
_____ __ | L: _____
_____ __ | D: _____

Mid-Day Habits | Water
_____ __ | ☐ ☐ ☐ ☐
_____ __ | ☐ ☐ ☐ ☐
_____ __ |

PM Habits | To Do's
_____ __ | _____ __
_____ __ | _____ __
_____ __ | _____ __

Affirmation:

Tuesday _____

AM Habits | Meals
_____ __ | B: _____
_____ __ | L: _____
_____ __ | D: _____

Mid-Day Habits | Water
_____ __ | ☐ ☐ ☐ ☐
_____ __ | ☐ ☐ ☐ ☐
_____ __ |

PM Habits | To Do's
_____ __ | _____ __
_____ __ | _____ __
_____ __ | _____ __

Wednesday _____

AM Habits | Meals
_____ __ | B: _____
_____ __ | L: _____
_____ __ | D: _____

Mid-Day Habits | Water
_____ __ | ☐ ☐ ☐ ☐
_____ __ | ☐ ☐ ☐ ☐
_____ __ |

PM Habits | To Do's
_____ __ | _____ __
_____ __ | _____ __
_____ __ | _____ __

♥

Monthly intention:

Thursday _____

AM Habits   Meals
_____ __   B: _____
_____ __   L: _____
_____ __   D:_____

Mid-Day Habits   Water
_____ __   ☐ ☐ ☐ ☐
_____ __   ☐ ☐ ☐ ☐
_____ __

PM Habits   To Do's
_____ __   _____ __
_____ __   _____ __
_____ __   _____ __

Friday _____

AM Habits   Meals
_____ __   B: _____
_____ __   L: _____
_____ __   D:_____

Mid-Day Habits   Water
_____ __   ☐ ☐ ☐ ☐
_____ __   ☐ ☐ ☐ ☐
_____ __

PM Habits   To Do's
_____ __   _____ __
_____ __   _____ __
_____ __   _____ __

Affirmation:

Saturday _____

AM Habits   Meals
_____ __   B: _____
_____ __   L: _____
_____ __   D:_____

Mid-Day Habits   Water
_____ __   ☐ ☐ ☐ ☐
_____ __   ☐ ☐ ☐ ☐
_____ __

PM Habits   To Do's
_____ __   _____ __
_____ __   _____ __
_____ __   _____ __

Space to Clear Your Mind

Weekly focus:

Sunday _____

AM Habits	Meals
_____ __	B: _____
_____ __	L: _____
_____ __	D: _____

Mid-Day Habits	Water
_____ __	☐ ☐ ☐ ☐
_____ __	☐ ☐ ☐ ☐
_____ __	

PM Habits	To Do's
_____ __	_____ __
_____ __	_____ __
_____ __	_____ __

Monday _____

AM Habits	Meals
_____ __	B: _____
_____ __	L: _____
_____ __	D: _____

Mid-Day Habits	Water
_____ __	☐ ☐ ☐ ☐
_____ __	☐ ☐ ☐ ☐
_____ __	

PM Habits	To Do's
_____ __	_____ __
_____ __	_____ __
_____ __	_____ __

Affirmation:

Tuesday _____

AM Habits	Meals
_____ __	B: _____
_____ __	L: _____
_____ __	D: _____

Mid-Day Habits	Water
_____ __	☐ ☐ ☐ ☐
_____ __	☐ ☐ ☐ ☐
_____ __	

PM Habits	To Do's
_____ __	_____ __
_____ __	_____ __
_____ __	_____ __

Wednesday _____

AM Habits	Meals
_____ __	B: _____
_____ __	L: _____
_____ __	D: _____

Mid-Day Habits	Water
_____ __	☐ ☐ ☐ ☐
_____ __	☐ ☐ ☐ ☐
_____ __	

PM Habits	To Do's
_____ __	_____ __
_____ __	_____ __
_____ __	_____ __

Monthly intention:

Thursday _____

AM Habits   Meals
_____ __   B: _____
_____ __   L: _____
_____ __   D:_____

Mid-Day Habits   Water
_____ __   ☐ ☐ ☐ ☐
_____ __   ☐ ☐ ☐ ☐
_____ __

PM Habits   To Do's
_____ __   _____ __
_____ __   _____ __
_____ __   _____ __

Friday _____

AM Habits   Meals
_____ __   B: _____
_____ __   L: _____
_____ __   D:_____

Mid-Day Habits   Water
_____ __   ☐ ☐ ☐ ☐
_____ __   ☐ ☐ ☐ ☐
_____ __

PM Habits   To Do's
_____ __   _____ __
_____ __   _____ __
_____ __   _____ __

Affirmation:

Saturday _____   Space to Clear Your Mind

AM Habits   Meals
_____ __   B: _____
_____ __   L: _____
_____ __   D:_____

Mid-Day Habits   Water
_____ __   ☐ ☐ ☐ ☐
_____ __   ☐ ☐ ☐ ☐
_____ __

PM Habits   To Do's
_____ __   _____ __
_____ __   _____ __
_____ __   _____ __

♥

Weekly focus:

Sunday _____

AM Habits   Meals
_____ __   B: _____
_____ __   L: _____
_____ __   D:_____

Mid-Day Habits   Water
_____ __   ☐ ☐ ☐ ☐
_____ __   ☐ ☐ ☐ ☐
_____ __

PM Habits   To Do's
_____ __   _____ __
_____ __   _____ __
_____ __   _____ __

Monday _____

AM Habits   Meals
_____ __   B: _____
_____ __   L: _____
_____ __   D:_____

Mid-Day Habits   Water
_____ __   ☐ ☐ ☐ ☐
_____ __   ☐ ☐ ☐ ☐
_____ __

PM Habits   To Do's
_____ __   _____ __
_____ __   _____ __
_____ __   _____ __

Affirmation:

Tuesday _____

AM Habits   Meals
_____ __   B: _____
_____ __   L: _____
_____ __   D:_____

Mid-Day Habits   Water
_____ __   ☐ ☐ ☐ ☐
_____ __   ☐ ☐ ☐ ☐

PM Habits   To Do's
_____ __   _____ __
_____ __   _____ __
_____ __   _____ __

Wednesday _____

AM Habits   Meals
_____ __   B: _____
_____ __   L: _____
_____ __   D:_____

Mid-Day Habits   Water
_____ __   ☐ ☐ ☐ ☐
_____ __   ☐ ☐ ☐ ☐

PM Habits   To Do's
_____ __   _____ __
_____ __   _____ __
_____ __   _____ __

Monthly intention:

Thursday _____

AM Habits

Meals

_____ __

B: _____

_____ __

L: _____

_____ __

D:_____

Mid-Day Habits

Water

_____ __

☐ ☐ ☐ ☐

_____ __

☐ ☐ ☐ ☐

_____ __

PM Habits

To Do's

_____ __

_____ __

_____ __

_____ __

_____ __

_____ __

Friday _____

AM Habits

Meals

_____ __

B: _____

_____ __

L: _____

_____ __

D:_____

Mid-Day Habits

Water

_____ __

☐ ☐ ☐ ☐

_____ __

☐ ☐ ☐ ☐

_____ __

PM Habits

To Do's

_____ __

_____ __

_____ __

_____ __

_____ __

_____ __

Affirmation:

Saturday _____

Space to Clear Your Mind

AM Habits

Meals

_____ __

B: _____

_____ __

L: _____

_____ __

D:_____

Mid-Day Habits

Water

_____ __

☐ ☐ ☐ ☐

_____ __

☐ ☐ ☐ ☐

_____ __

PM Habits

To Do's

_____ __

_____ __

_____ __

_____ __

_____ __

_____ __

Weekly focus:

Sunday _____

AM Habits	Meals
_____ __	B: _____
_____ __	L: _____
_____ __	D:_____

Mid-Day Habits   Water

_____ __   ☐ ☐ ☐ ☐
_____ __   ☐ ☐ ☐ ☐
_____ __

PM Habits   To Do's

_____ __   _____ __
_____ __   _____ __
_____ __   _____ __

Monday _____

AM Habits	Meals
_____ __	B: _____
_____ __	L: _____
_____ __	D:_____

Mid-Day Habits   Water

_____ __   ☐ ☐ ☐ ☐
_____ __   ☐ ☐ ☐ ☐
_____ __

PM Habits   To Do's

_____ __   _____ __
_____ __   _____ __
_____ __   _____ __

Affirmation:

Tuesday _____

AM Habits	Meals
_____ __	B: _____
_____ __	L: _____
_____ __	D:_____

Mid-Day Habits   Water

_____ __   ☐ ☐ ☐ ☐
_____ __   ☐ ☐ ☐ ☐
_____ __

PM Habits   To Do's

_____ __   _____ __
_____ __   _____ __
_____ __   _____ __

Wednesday _____

AM Habits	Meals
_____ __	B: _____
_____ __	L: _____
_____ __	D:_____

Mid-Day Habits   Water

_____ __   ☐ ☐ ☐ ☐
_____ __   ☐ ☐ ☐ ☐
_____ __

PM Habits   To Do's

_____ __   _____ __
_____ __   _____ __
_____ __   _____ __

♥

Monthly intention:

Thursday _____

AM Habits   Meals
_____ __   B: _____
_____ __   L: _____
_____ __   D:_____

Mid-Day Habits   Water
_____ __   ☐ ☐ ☐ ☐
_____ __   ☐ ☐ ☐ ☐
_____ __

PM Habits   To Do's
_____ __   _____ __
_____ __   _____ __
_____ __   _____ __

Friday _____

AM Habits   Meals
_____ __   B: _____
_____ __   L: _____
_____ __   D:_____

Mid-Day Habits   Water
_____ __   ☐ ☐ ☐ ☐
_____ __   ☐ ☐ ☐ ☐
_____ __

PM Habits   To Do's
_____ __   _____ __
_____ __   _____ __
_____ __   _____ __

Affirmation:

Saturday _____

AM Habits   Meals
_____ __   B: _____
_____ __   L: _____
_____ __   D:_____

Mid-Day Habits   Water
_____ __   ☐ ☐ ☐ ☐
_____ __   ☐ ☐ ☐ ☐
_____ __

PM Habits   To Do's
_____ __   _____ __
_____ __   _____ __
_____ __   _____ __

Space to Clear Your Mind

Weekly focus:

Sunday _____

AM Habits	Meals
_____ __	B: _____
_____ __	L: _____
_____ __	D: _____

Mid-Day Habits	Water
_____ __	☐ ☐ ☐ ☐
_____ __	☐ ☐ ☐ ☐
_____ __	

PM Habits	To Do's
_____ __	_____ __
_____ __	_____ __
_____ __	_____ __

Monday _____

AM Habits	Meals
_____ __	B: _____
_____ __	L: _____
_____ __	D: _____

Mid-Day Habits	Water
_____ __	☐ ☐ ☐ ☐
_____ __	☐ ☐ ☐ ☐
_____ __	

PM Habits	To Do's
_____ __	_____ __
_____ __	_____ __
_____ __	_____ __

Affirmation:

Tuesday _____

AM Habits	Meals
_____ __	B: _____
_____ __	L: _____
_____ __	D: _____

Mid-Day Habits	Water
_____ __	☐ ☐ ☐ ☐
_____ __	☐ ☐ ☐ ☐
_____ __	

PM Habits	To Do's
_____ __	_____ __
_____ __	_____ __
_____ __	_____ __

Wednesday _____

AM Habits	Meals
_____ __	B: _____
_____ __	L: _____
_____ __	D: _____

Mid-Day Habits	Water
_____ __	☐ ☐ ☐ ☐
_____ __	☐ ☐ ☐ ☐
_____ __	

PM Habits	To Do's
_____ __	_____ __
_____ __	_____ __
_____ __	_____ __

Monthly intention:

Thursday _____

AM Habits   Meals
_____ __   B: _____
_____ __   L: _____
_____ __   D:_____

Mid-Day Habits   Water
_____ __   ☐ ☐ ☐ ☐
_____ __   ☐ ☐ ☐ ☐

PM Habits   To Do's
_____ __   _____ __
_____ __   _____ __
_____ __   _____ __

Friday _____

AM Habits   Meals
_____ __   B: _____
_____ __   L: _____
_____ __   D:_____

Mid-Day Habits   Water
_____ __   ☐ ☐ ☐ ☐
_____ __   ☐ ☐ ☐ ☐

PM Habits   To Do's
_____ __   _____ __
_____ __   _____ __
_____ __   _____ __

Affirmation:

Saturday _____

AM Habits   Meals
_____ __   B: _____
_____ __   L: _____
_____ __   D:_____

Mid-Day Habits   Water
_____ __   ☐ ☐ ☐ ☐
_____ __   ☐ ☐ ☐ ☐

PM Habits   To Do's
_____ __   _____ __
_____ __   _____ __
_____ __   _____ __

Space to Clear Your Mind

Weekly focus:

Sunday _____

AM Habits	Meals
_____ __	B: _____
_____ __	L: _____
_____ __	D:_____

Mid-Day Habits   Water

_____ __   ☐ ☐ ☐ ☐
_____ __   ☐ ☐ ☐ ☐
_____ __

PM Habits	To Do's
_____ __	_____ __
_____ __	_____ __
_____ __	_____ __

Monday _____

AM Habits	Meals
_____ __	B: _____
_____ __	L: _____
_____ __	D:_____

Mid-Day Habits   Water

_____ __   ☐ ☐ ☐ ☐
_____ __   ☐ ☐ ☐ ☐
_____ __

PM Habits	To Do's
_____ __	_____ __
_____ __	_____ __
_____ __	_____ __

Affirmation:

Tuesday _____

AM Habits	Meals
_____ __	B: _____
_____ __	L: _____
_____ __	D:_____

Mid-Day Habits   Water

_____ __   ☐ ☐ ☐ ☐
_____ __   ☐ ☐ ☐ ☐

PM Habits	To Do's
_____ __	_____ __
_____ __	_____ __
_____ __	_____ __

Wednesday _____

AM Habits	Meals
_____ __	B: _____
_____ __	L: _____
_____ __	D:_____

Mid-Day Habits   Water

_____ __   ☐ ☐ ☐ ☐
_____ __   ☐ ☐ ☐ ☐

PM Habits	To Do's
_____ __	_____ __
_____ __	_____ __
_____ __	_____ __

Monthly intention:

Thursday _____

AM Habits   Meals
_____ __   B: _____
_____ __   L: _____
_____ __   D:_____

Mid-Day Habits   Water
_____ __   ☐ ☐ ☐ ☐
_____ __   ☐ ☐ ☐ ☐
_____ __

PM Habits   To Do's
_____ __   _____ __
_____ __   _____ __
_____ __   _____ __

Friday _____

AM Habits   Meals
_____ __   B: _____
_____ __   L: _____
_____ __   D:_____

Mid-Day Habits   Water
_____ __   ☐ ☐ ☐ ☐
_____ __   ☐ ☐ ☐ ☐
_____ __

PM Habits   To Do's
_____ __   _____ __
_____ __   _____ __
_____ __   _____ __

Affirmation:

Saturday _____

AM Habits   Meals
_____ __   B: _____
_____ __   L: _____
_____ __   D:_____

Mid-Day Habits   Water
_____ __   ☐ ☐ ☐ ☐
_____ __   ☐ ☐ ☐ ☐
_____ __

PM Habits   To Do's
_____ __   _____ __
_____ __   _____ __
_____ __   _____ __

Space to Clear Your Mind

Weekly focus:

Sunday _____

AM Habits   Meals
_____ __   B: _____
_____ __   L: _____
_____ __   D:_____

Mid-Day Habits   Water
_____ __   ☐ ☐ ☐ ☐
_____ __   ☐ ☐ ☐ ☐
_____ __

PM Habits   To Do's
_____ __   _____ __
_____ __   _____ __
_____ __   _____ __

Monday _____

AM Habits   Meals
_____ __   B: _____
_____ __   L: _____
_____ __   D:_____

Mid-Day Habits   Water
_____ __   ☐ ☐ ☐ ☐
_____ __   ☐ ☐ ☐ ☐
_____ __

PM Habits   To Do's
_____ __   _____ __
_____ __   _____ __
_____ __   _____ __

Affirmation:

Tuesday _____

AM Habits   Meals
_____ __   B: _____
_____ __   L: _____
_____ __   D:_____

Mid-Day Habits   Water
_____ __   ☐ ☐ ☐ ☐
_____ __   ☐ ☐ ☐ ☐
_____ __

PM Habits   To Do's
_____ __   _____ __
_____ __   _____ __
_____ __   _____ __

Wednesday _____

AM Habits   Meals
_____ __   B: _____
_____ __   L: _____
_____ __   D:_____

Mid-Day Habits   Water
_____ __   ☐ ☐ ☐ ☐
_____ __   ☐ ☐ ☐ ☐
_____ __

PM Habits   To Do's
_____ __   _____ __
_____ __   _____ __
_____ __   _____ __

Monthly intention:

Thursday _____

AM Habits   Meals
_____ __   B: _____
_____ __   L: _____
_____ __   D:_____

Mid-Day Habits   Water
_____ __   ☐ ☐ ☐ ☐
_____ __   ☐ ☐ ☐ ☐
_____ __

PM Habits   To Do's
_____ __   _____ __
_____ __   _____ __
_____ __   _____ __

Friday _____

AM Habits   Meals
_____ __   B: _____
_____ __   L: _____
_____ __   D:_____

Mid-Day Habits   Water
_____ __   ☐ ☐ ☐ ☐
_____ __   ☐ ☐ ☐ ☐
_____ __

PM Habits   To Do's
_____ __   _____ __
_____ __   _____ __
_____ __   _____ __

Affirmation:

Saturday _____   Space to Clear Your Mind

AM Habits   Meals
_____ __   B: _____
_____ __   L: _____
_____ __   D:_____

Mid-Day Habits   Water
_____ __   ☐ ☐ ☐ ☐
_____ __   ☐ ☐ ☐ ☐
_____ __

PM Habits   To Do's
_____ __   _____ __
_____ __   _____ __
_____ __   _____ __

Weekly focus:

Sunday _____

AM Habits	Meals
_____ __	B: _____
_____ __	L: _____
_____ __	D:_____

Mid-Day Habits	Water
_____ __	☐ ☐ ☐ ☐
_____ __	☐ ☐ ☐ ☐
_____ __	

PM Habits	To Do's
_____ __	_____ __
_____ __	_____ __
_____ __	_____ __

Monday _____

AM Habits	Meals
_____ __	B: _____
_____ __	L: _____
_____ __	D:_____

Mid-Day Habits	Water
_____ __	☐ ☐ ☐ ☐
_____ __	☐ ☐ ☐ ☐
_____ __	

PM Habits	To Do's
_____ __	_____ __
_____ __	_____ __
_____ __	_____ __

Affirmation:

Tuesday _____

AM Habits	Meals
_____ __	B: _____
_____ __	L: _____
_____ __	D:_____

Mid-Day Habits	Water
_____ __	☐ ☐ ☐ ☐
_____ __	☐ ☐ ☐ ☐
_____ __	

PM Habits	To Do's
_____ __	_____ __
_____ __	_____ __
_____ __	_____ __

Wednesday _____

AM Habits	Meals
_____ __	B: _____
_____ __	L: _____
_____ __	D:_____

Mid-Day Habits	Water
_____ __	☐ ☐ ☐ ☐
_____ __	☐ ☐ ☐ ☐
_____ __	

PM Habits	To Do's
_____ __	_____ __
_____ __	_____ __
_____ __	_____ __

Monthly intention:

Thursday _____

AM Habits   Meals
_____ __   B: _____
_____ __   L: _____
_____ __   D:_____

Mid-Day Habits   Water
_____ __   ☐ ☐ ☐ ☐
_____ __   ☐ ☐ ☐ ☐

PM Habits   To Do's
_____ __   _____ __
_____ __   _____ __
_____ __   _____ __

Friday _____

AM Habits   Meals
_____ __   B: _____
_____ __   L: _____
_____ __   D:_____

Mid-Day Habits   Water
_____ __   ☐ ☐ ☐ ☐
_____ __   ☐ ☐ ☐ ☐

PM Habits   To Do's
_____ __   _____ __
_____ __   _____ __
_____ __   _____ __

Affirmation:

Saturday _____   Space to Clear Your Mind

AM Habits   Meals
_____ __   B: _____
_____ __   L: _____
_____ __   D:_____

Mid-Day Habits   Water
_____ __   ☐ ☐ ☐ ☐
_____ __   ☐ ☐ ☐ ☐

PM Habits   To Do's
_____ __   _____ __
_____ __   _____ __
_____ __   _____ __

Weekly focus:

Sunday _____

AM Habits   Meals
_____ __   B: _____
_____ __   L: _____
_____ __   D: _____

Mid-Day Habits   Water
_____ __   ☐ ☐ ☐ ☐
_____ __   ☐ ☐ ☐ ☐
_____ __

PM Habits   To Do's
_____ __   _____ __
_____ __   _____ __
_____ __   _____ __

Monday _____

AM Habits   Meals
_____ __   B: _____
_____ __   L: _____
_____ __   D: _____

Mid-Day Habits   Water
_____ __   ☐ ☐ ☐ ☐
_____ __   ☐ ☐ ☐ ☐
_____ __

PM Habits   To Do's
_____ __   _____ __
_____ __   _____ __
_____ __   _____ __

Affirmation:

Tuesday _____

AM Habits   Meals
_____ __   B: _____
_____ __   L: _____
_____ __   D: _____

Mid-Day Habits   Water
_____ __   ☐ ☐ ☐ ☐
_____ __   ☐ ☐ ☐ ☐
_____ __

PM Habits   To Do's
_____ __   _____ __
_____ __   _____ __
_____ __   _____ __

Wednesday _____

AM Habits   Meals
_____ __   B: _____
_____ __   L: _____
_____ __   D: _____

Mid-Day Habits   Water
_____ __   ☐ ☐ ☐ ☐
_____ __   ☐ ☐ ☐ ☐
_____ __

PM Habits   To Do's
_____ __   _____ __
_____ __   _____ __
_____ __   _____ __

Monthly intention:

Thursday _____

AM Habits   Meals
_____ __   B: _____
_____ __   L: _____
_____ __   D:_____

Mid-Day Habits   Water
_____ __   ☐ ☐ ☐ ☐
_____ __   ☐ ☐ ☐ ☐
_____ __

PM Habits   To Do's
_____ __   _____ __
_____ __   _____ __
_____ __   _____ __

Friday _____

AM Habits   Meals
_____ __   B: _____
_____ __   L: _____
_____ __   D:_____

Mid-Day Habits   Water
_____ __   ☐ ☐ ☐ ☐
_____ __   ☐ ☐ ☐ ☐
_____ __

PM Habits   To Do's
_____ __   _____ __
_____ __   _____ __
_____ __   _____ __

Affirmation:

Saturday _____

AM Habits   Meals
_____ __   B: _____
_____ __   L: _____
_____ __   D:_____

Mid-Day Habits   Water
_____ __   ☐ ☐ ☐ ☐
_____ __   ☐ ☐ ☐ ☐
_____ __

PM Habits   To Do's
_____ __   _____ __
_____ __   _____ __
_____ __   _____ __

Space to Clear Your Mind

Weekly focus:

Sunday _____

AM Habits   Meals
_____ __   B: _____
_____ __   L: _____
_____ __   D:_____

Mid-Day Habits   Water
_____ __   ☐ ☐ ☐ ☐
_____ __   ☐ ☐ ☐ ☐
_____ __

PM Habits   To Do's
_____ __   _____ __
_____ __   _____ __
_____ __   _____ __

Monday _____

AM Habits   Meals
_____ __   B: _____
_____ __   L: _____
_____ __   D:_____

Mid-Day Habits   Water
_____ __   ☐ ☐ ☐ ☐
_____ __   ☐ ☐ ☐ ☐
_____ __

PM Habits   To Do's
_____ __   _____ __
_____ __   _____ __
_____ __   _____ __

Affirmation:

Tuesday _____

AM Habits   Meals
_____ __   B: _____
_____ __   L: _____
_____ __   D:_____

Mid-Day Habits   Water
_____ __   ☐ ☐ ☐ ☐
_____ __   ☐ ☐ ☐ ☐
_____ __

PM Habits   To Do's
_____ __   _____ __
_____ __   _____ __
_____ __   _____ __

Wednesday _____

AM Habits   Meals
_____ __   B: _____
_____ __   L: _____
_____ __   D:_____

Mid-Day Habits   Water
_____ __   ☐ ☐ ☐ ☐
_____ __   ☐ ☐ ☐ ☐
_____ __

PM Habits   To Do's
_____ __   _____ __
_____ __   _____ __
_____ __   _____ __

Monthly intention:

Thursday _____

AM Habits   Meals
_____ __   B: _____
_____ __   L: _____
_____ __   D: _____

Mid-Day Habits   Water
_____ __   ☐ ☐ ☐ ☐
_____ __   ☐ ☐ ☐ ☐
_____ __

PM Habits   To Do's
_____ __   _____ __
_____ __   _____ __
_____ __   _____ __

Friday _____

AM Habits   Meals
_____ __   B: _____
_____ __   L: _____
_____ __   D: _____

Mid-Day Habits   Water
_____ __   ☐ ☐ ☐ ☐
_____ __   ☐ ☐ ☐ ☐
_____ __

PM Habits   To Do's
_____ __   _____ __
_____ __   _____ __
_____ __   _____ __

Affirmation:

Saturday _____   Space to Clear Your Mind

AM Habits   Meals
_____ __   B: _____
_____ __   L: _____
_____ __   D: _____

Mid-Day Habits   Water
_____ __   ☐ ☐ ☐ ☐
_____ __   ☐ ☐ ☐ ☐
_____ __

PM Habits   To Do's
_____ __   _____ __
_____ __   _____ __
_____ __   _____ __

Weekly focus:

Sunday _____

AM Habits   Meals
_____ __   B: _____
_____ __   L: _____
_____ __   D:_____

Mid-Day Habits   Water
_____ __   ☐ ☐ ☐ ☐
_____ __   ☐ ☐ ☐ ☐
_____ __

PM Habits   To Do's
_____ __   _____ __
_____ __   _____ __
_____ __   _____ __

Monday _____

AM Habits   Meals
_____ __   B: _____
_____ __   L: _____
_____ __   D:_____

Mid-Day Habits   Water
_____ __   ☐ ☐ ☐ ☐
_____ __   ☐ ☐ ☐ ☐
_____ __

PM Habits   To Do's
_____ __   _____ __
_____ __   _____ __
_____ __   _____ __

Affirmation:

Tuesday _____

AM Habits   Meals
_____ __   B: _____
_____ __   L: _____
_____ __   D:_____

Mid-Day Habits   Water
_____ __   ☐ ☐ ☐ ☐
_____ __   ☐ ☐ ☐ ☐
_____ __

PM Habits   To Do's
_____ __   _____ __
_____ __   _____ __
_____ __   _____ __

Wednesday _____

AM Habits   Meals
_____ __   B: _____
_____ __   L: _____
_____ __   D:_____

Mid-Day Habits   Water
_____ __   ☐ ☐ ☐ ☐
_____ __   ☐ ☐ ☐ ☐
_____ __

PM Habits   To Do's
_____ __   _____ __
_____ __   _____ __
_____ __   _____ __

Monthly intention:

Thursday _____

AM Habits   Meals
_____ __   B: _____
_____ __   L: _____
_____ __   D:_____

Mid-Day Habits   Water
_____ __   ☐ ☐ ☐ ☐
_____ __   ☐ ☐ ☐ ☐

PM Habits   To Do's
_____ __   _____ __
_____ __   _____ __
_____ __   _____ __

Friday _____

AM Habits   Meals
_____ __   B: _____
_____ __   L: _____
_____ __   D:_____

Mid-Day Habits   Water
_____ __   ☐ ☐ ☐ ☐
_____ __   ☐ ☐ ☐ ☐

PM Habits   To Do's
_____ __   _____ __
_____ __   _____ __
_____ __   _____ __

Affirmation:

Saturday _____

AM Habits   Meals
_____ __   B: _____
_____ __   L: _____
_____ __   D:_____

Mid-Day Habits   Water
_____ __   ☐ ☐ ☐ ☐
_____ __   ☐ ☐ ☐ ☐

PM Habits   To Do's
_____ __   _____ __
_____ __   _____ __
_____ __   _____ __

Space to Clear Your Mind

Weekly focus:

Sunday _____

AM Habits

_____ __
_____ __
_____ __

Meals

B: _____
L: _____
D:_____

Mid-Day Habits

_____ __
_____ __
_____ __

Water

☐ ☐ ☐ ☐
☐ ☐ ☐ ☐

PM Habits

_____ __
_____ __
_____ __

To Do's

_____ __
_____ __
_____ __

Monday _____

AM Habits

_____ __
_____ __
_____ __

Meals

B: _____
L: _____
D:_____

Mid-Day Habits

_____ __
_____ __
_____ __

Water

☐ ☐ ☐ ☐
☐ ☐ ☐ ☐

PM Habits

_____ __
_____ __
_____ __

To Do's

_____ __
_____ __
_____ __

Affirmation:

Tuesday _____

AM Habits

_____ __
_____ __
_____ __

Meals

B: _____
L: _____
D:_____

Mid-Day Habits

_____ __
_____ __
_____ __

Water

☐ ☐ ☐ ☐
☐ ☐ ☐ ☐

PM Habits

_____ __
_____ __
_____ __

To Do's

_____ __
_____ __
_____ __

Wednesday _____

AM Habits

_____ __
_____ __
_____ __

Meals

B: _____
L: _____
D:_____

Mid-Day Habits

_____ __
_____ __
_____ __

Water

☐ ☐ ☐ ☐
☐ ☐ ☐ ☐

PM Habits

_____ __
_____ __
_____ __

To Do's

_____ __
_____ __
_____ __

Monthly intention:

Thursday _____

AM Habits   Meals
_____ __   B: _____
_____ __   L: _____
_____ __   D: _____

Mid-Day Habits   Water
_____ __   ☐ ☐ ☐ ☐
_____ __   ☐ ☐ ☐ ☐
_____ __

PM Habits   To Do's
_____ __   _____ __
_____ __   _____ __
_____ __   _____ __

Friday _____

AM Habits   Meals
_____ __   B: _____
_____ __   L: _____
_____ __   D: _____

Mid-Day Habits   Water
_____ __   ☐ ☐ ☐ ☐
_____ __   ☐ ☐ ☐ ☐
_____ __

PM Habits   To Do's
_____ __   _____ __
_____ __   _____ __
_____ __   _____ __

Affirmation:

Saturday _____

AM Habits   Meals
_____ __   B: _____
_____ __   L: _____
_____ __   D: _____

Mid-Day Habits   Water
_____ __   ☐ ☐ ☐ ☐
_____ __   ☐ ☐ ☐ ☐
_____ __

PM Habits   To Do's
_____ __   _____ __
_____ __   _____ __
_____ __   _____ __

Space to Clear Your Mind

Weekly focus:

Sunday _____

AM Habits	Meals
_____ __	B: _____
_____ __	L: _____
_____ __	D: _____

Mid-Day Habits	Water
_____ __	☐ ☐ ☐ ☐
_____ __	☐ ☐ ☐ ☐
_____ __	

PM Habits	To Do's
_____ __	_____ __
_____ __	_____ __
_____ __	_____ __

Monday _____

AM Habits	Meals
_____ __	B: _____
_____ __	L: _____
_____ __	D: _____

Mid-Day Habits	Water
_____ __	☐ ☐ ☐ ☐
_____ __	☐ ☐ ☐ ☐
_____ __	

PM Habits	To Do's
_____ __	_____ __
_____ __	_____ __
_____ __	_____ __

Affirmation:

Tuesday _____

AM Habits	Meals
_____ __	B: _____
_____ __	L: _____
_____ __	D: _____

Mid-Day Habits	Water
_____ __	☐ ☐ ☐ ☐
_____ __	☐ ☐ ☐ ☐
_____ __	

PM Habits	To Do's
_____ __	_____ __
_____ __	_____ __
_____ __	_____ __

Wednesday _____

AM Habits	Meals
_____ __	B: _____
_____ __	L: _____
_____ __	D: _____

Mid-Day Habits	Water
_____ __	☐ ☐ ☐ ☐
_____ __	☐ ☐ ☐ ☐
_____ __	

PM Habits	To Do's
_____ __	_____ __
_____ __	_____ __
_____ __	_____ __

Monthly intention:

Thursday _____   Friday _____

AM Habits   Meals   AM Habits   Meals
_____ __   B: _____   _____ __   B: _____
_____ __   L: _____   _____ __   L: _____
_____ __   D: _____   _____ __   D: _____

Mid-Day Habits   Water   Mid-Day Habits   Water
_____ __   ☐ ☐ ☐ ☐   _____ __   ☐ ☐ ☐ ☐
_____ __   ☐ ☐ ☐ ☐   _____ __   ☐ ☐ ☐ ☐

PM Habits   To Do's   PM Habits   To Do's
_____ __   _____ __   _____ __   _____ __
_____ __   _____ __   _____ __   _____ __
_____ __   _____ __   _____ __   _____ __

Affirmation:

Saturday _____   Space to Clear Your Mind

AM Habits   Meals
_____ __   B: _____
_____ __   L: _____
_____ __   D: _____

Mid-Day Habits   Water
_____ __   ☐ ☐ ☐ ☐
_____ __   ☐ ☐ ☐ ☐

PM Habits   To Do's
_____ __   _____ __
_____ __   _____ __
_____ __   _____ __

Weekly focus:

Sunday _____

AM Habits	Meals
_____ __	B: _____
_____ __	L: _____
_____ __	D: _____

Mid-Day Habits	Water
_____ __	☐ ☐ ☐ ☐
_____ __	☐ ☐ ☐ ☐
_____ __	

PM Habits	To Do's
_____ __	_____ __
_____ __	_____ __
_____ __	_____ __

Monday _____

AM Habits	Meals
_____ __	B: _____
_____ __	L: _____
_____ __	D: _____

Mid-Day Habits	Water
_____ __	☐ ☐ ☐ ☐
_____ __	☐ ☐ ☐ ☐
_____ __	

PM Habits	To Do's
_____ __	_____ __
_____ __	_____ __
_____ __	_____ __

Affirmation:

Tuesday _____

AM Habits	Meals
_____ __	B: _____
_____ __	L: _____
_____ __	D: _____

Mid-Day Habits	Water
_____ __	☐ ☐ ☐ ☐
_____ __	☐ ☐ ☐ ☐
_____ __	

PM Habits	To Do's
_____ __	_____ __
_____ __	_____ __
_____ __	_____ __

Wednesday _____

AM Habits	Meals
_____ __	B: _____
_____ __	L: _____
_____ __	D: _____

Mid-Day Habits	Water
_____ __	☐ ☐ ☐ ☐
_____ __	☐ ☐ ☐ ☐
_____ __	

PM Habits	To Do's
_____ __	_____ __
_____ __	_____ __
_____ __	_____ __

Monthly intention:

Thursday _____

AM Habits _____ __

Meals
B: _____
L: _____
D: _____

Mid-Day Habits _____ __

Water
☐ ☐ ☐ ☐
☐ ☐ ☐ ☐

PM Habits
_____ __
_____ __
_____ __

To Do's
_____ __
_____ __
_____ __

Friday _____

AM Habits _____ __

Meals
B: _____
L: _____
D: _____

Mid-Day Habits _____ __

Water
☐ ☐ ☐ ☐
☐ ☐ ☐ ☐

PM Habits
_____ __
_____ __
_____ __

To Do's
_____ __
_____ __
_____ __

Affirmation:

Saturday _____

AM Habits _____ __

Meals
B: _____
L: _____
D: _____

Mid-Day Habits _____ __

Water
☐ ☐ ☐ ☐
☐ ☐ ☐ ☐

PM Habits
_____ __
_____ __
_____ __

To Do's
_____ __
_____ __
_____ __

Space to Clear Your Mind

Weekly focus:

Sunday _____

AM Habits   Meals
_____ __   B: _____
_____ __   L: _____
_____ __   D:_____

Mid-Day Habits   Water
_____ __   ☐ ☐ ☐ ☐
_____ __   ☐ ☐ ☐ ☐
_____ __

PM Habits   To Do's
_____ __   _____ __
_____ __   _____ __
_____ __   _____ __

Monday _____

AM Habits   Meals
_____ __   B: _____
_____ __   L: _____
_____ __   D:_____

Mid-Day Habits   Water
_____ __   ☐ ☐ ☐ ☐
_____ __   ☐ ☐ ☐ ☐
_____ __

PM Habits   To Do's
_____ __   _____ __
_____ __   _____ __
_____ __   _____ __

Affirmation:

Tuesday _____

AM Habits   Meals
_____ __   B: _____
_____ __   L: _____
_____ __   D:_____

Mid-Day Habits   Water
_____ __   ☐ ☐ ☐ ☐
_____ __   ☐ ☐ ☐ ☐
_____ __

PM Habits   To Do's
_____ __   _____ __
_____ __   _____ __
_____ __   _____ __

Wednesday _____

AM Habits   Meals
_____ __   B: _____
_____ __   L: _____
_____ __   D:_____

Mid-Day Habits   Water
_____ __   ☐ ☐ ☐ ☐
_____ __   ☐ ☐ ☐ ☐
_____ __

PM Habits   To Do's
_____ __   _____ __
_____ __   _____ __
_____ __   _____ __

Monthly intention:

Thursday _____

AM Habits	Meals
_____ __	B: _____
_____ __	L: _____
_____ __	D:_____

Mid-Day Habits Water

☐ ☐ ☐ ☐
☐ ☐ ☐ ☐

PM Habits To Do's

_____ __   _____ __
_____ __   _____ __
_____ __   _____ __

Friday _____

AM Habits	Meals
_____ __	B: _____
_____ __	L: _____
_____ __	D:_____

Mid-Day Habits Water

☐ ☐ ☐ ☐
☐ ☐ ☐ ☐

PM Habits To Do's

_____ __   _____ __
_____ __   _____ __
_____ __   _____ __

Affirmation:

Saturday _____

Space to Clear Your Mind

AM Habits	Meals
_____ __	B: _____
_____ __	L: _____
_____ __	D:_____

Mid-Day Habits Water

☐ ☐ ☐ ☐
☐ ☐ ☐ ☐

PM Habits To Do's

_____ __   _____ __
_____ __   _____ __
_____ __   _____ __

Weekly focus:

Sunday _____

AM Habits   Meals
_____ __ B: _____
_____ __ L: _____
_____ __ D:_____

Mid-Day Habits Water
_____ __ ☐ ☐ ☐ ☐
_____ __ ☐ ☐ ☐ ☐
_____ __

PM Habits To Do's
_____ __ _____ __
_____ __ _____ __
_____ __ _____ __

Monday _____

AM Habits   Meals
_____ __ B: _____
_____ __ L: _____
_____ __ D:_____

Mid-Day Habits Water
_____ __ ☐ ☐ ☐ ☐
_____ __ ☐ ☐ ☐ ☐

PM Habits To Do's
_____ __ _____ __
_____ __ _____ __
_____ __ _____ __

Affirmation:

Tuesday _____

AM Habits   Meals
_____ __ B: _____
_____ __ L: _____
_____ __ D:_____

Mid-Day Habits Water
_____ __ ☐ ☐ ☐ ☐
_____ __ ☐ ☐ ☐ ☐

PM Habits To Do's
_____ __ _____ __
_____ __ _____ __
_____ __ _____ __

Wednesday _____

AM Habits   Meals
_____ __ B: _____
_____ __ L: _____
_____ __ D:_____

Mid-Day Habits Water
_____ __ ☐ ☐ ☐ ☐
_____ __ ☐ ☐ ☐ ☐

PM Habits To Do's
_____ __ _____ __
_____ __ _____ __
_____ __ _____ __

Monthly intention:

Thursday _____

AM Habits   Meals
_____ __   B: _____
_____ __   L: _____
_____ __   D:_____

Mid-Day Habits   Water
_____ __   ☐ ☐ ☐ ☐
_____ __   ☐ ☐ ☐ ☐
_____ __

PM Habits   To Do's
_____ __   _____ __
_____ __   _____ __
_____ __   _____ __

Friday _____

AM Habits   Meals
_____ __   B: _____
_____ __   L: _____
_____ __   D:_____

Mid-Day Habits   Water
_____ __   ☐ ☐ ☐ ☐
_____ __   ☐ ☐ ☐ ☐
_____ __

PM Habits   To Do's
_____ __   _____ __
_____ __   _____ __
_____ __   _____ __

Affirmation:

Saturday _____

AM Habits   Meals
_____ __   B: _____
_____ __   L: _____
_____ __   D:_____

Mid-Day Habits   Water
_____ __   ☐ ☐ ☐ ☐
_____ __   ☐ ☐ ☐ ☐
_____ __

PM Habits   To Do's
_____ __   _____ __
_____ __   _____ __
_____ __   _____ __

Space to Clear Your Mind

Weekly focus:

Sunday _____

AM Habits   Meals
_____ __   B: _____
_____ __   L: _____
_____ __   D:_____

Mid-Day Habits   Water
_____ __   ☐ ☐ ☐ ☐
_____ __   ☐ ☐ ☐ ☐
_____ __

PM Habits   To Do's
_____ __   _____ __
_____ __   _____ __
_____ __   _____ __

Monday _____

AM Habits   Meals
_____ __   B: _____
_____ __   L: _____
_____ __   D:_____

Mid-Day Habits   Water
_____ __   ☐ ☐ ☐ ☐
_____ __   ☐ ☐ ☐ ☐
_____ __

PM Habits   To Do's
_____ __   _____ __
_____ __   _____ __
_____ __   _____ __

Affirmation:

Tuesday _____

AM Habits   Meals
_____ __   B: _____
_____ __   L: _____
_____ __   D:_____

Mid-Day Habits   Water
_____ __   ☐ ☐ ☐ ☐
_____ __   ☐ ☐ ☐ ☐
_____ __

PM Habits   To Do's
_____ __   _____ __
_____ __   _____ __
_____ __   _____ __

Wednesday _____

AM Habits   Meals
_____ __   B: _____
_____ __   L: _____
_____ __   D:_____

Mid-Day Habits   Water
_____ __   ☐ ☐ ☐ ☐
_____ __   ☐ ☐ ☐ ☐
_____ __

PM Habits   To Do's
_____ __   _____ __
_____ __   _____ __
_____ __   _____ __

Monthly intention:

Thursday _____

AM Habits   Meals
_____ __   B: _____
_____ __   L: _____
_____ __   D:_____

Mid-Day Habits   Water
_____ __   ☐ ☐ ☐ ☐
_____ __   ☐ ☐ ☐ ☐

PM Habits   To Do's
_____ __   _____ __
_____ __   _____ __
_____ __   _____ __

Friday _____

AM Habits   Meals
_____ __   B: _____
_____ __   L: _____
_____ __   D:_____

Mid-Day Habits   Water
_____ __   ☐ ☐ ☐ ☐
_____ __   ☐ ☐ ☐ ☐

PM Habits   To Do's
_____ __   _____ __
_____ __   _____ __
_____ __   _____ __

Affirmation:

Saturday _____

AM Habits   Meals
_____ __   B: _____
_____ __   L: _____
_____ __   D:_____

Mid-Day Habits   Water
_____ __   ☐ ☐ ☐ ☐
_____ __   ☐ ☐ ☐ ☐

PM Habits   To Do's
_____ __   _____ __
_____ __   _____ __
_____ __   _____ __

Space to Clear Your Mind

Weekly focus:

Sunday _____

AM Habits   Meals
_____ __   B: _____
_____ __   L: _____
_____ __   D:_____

Mid-Day Habits   Water
_____ _   ☐ ☐ ☐ ☐
_____ _   ☐ ☐ ☐ ☐
_____ _

PM Habits   To Do's
_____ __   _____ __
_____ __   _____ __
_____ __   _____ __

Monday _____

AM Habits   Meals
_____ __   B: _____
_____ __   L: _____
_____ __   D:_____

Mid-Day Habits   Water
_____ _   ☐ ☐ ☐ ☐
_____ _   ☐ ☐ ☐ ☐
_____ _

PM Habits   To Do's
_____ __   _____ __
_____ __   _____ __
_____ __   _____ __

Affirmation:

Tuesday _____

AM Habits   Meals
_____ __   B: _____
_____ __   L: _____
_____ __   D:_____

Mid-Day Habits   Water
_____ _   ☐ ☐ ☐ ☐
_____ _   ☐ ☐ ☐ ☐
_____ _

PM Habits   To Do's
_____ __   _____ __
_____ __   _____ __
_____ __   _____ __

Wednesday _____

AM Habits   Meals
_____ __   B: _____
_____ __   L: _____
_____ __   D:_____

Mid-Day Habits   Water
_____ _   ☐ ☐ ☐ ☐
_____ _   ☐ ☐ ☐ ☐
_____ _

PM Habits   To Do's
_____ __   _____ __
_____ __   _____ __
_____ __   _____ __

Monthly intention:

Thursday _____

AM Habits   Meals
_____ __   B: _____
_____ __   L: _____
_____ __   D:_____

Mid-Day Habits   Water
_____ __   ☐ ☐ ☐ ☐
_____ __   ☐ ☐ ☐ ☐
_____ __

PM Habits   To Do's
_____ __   _____ __
_____ __   _____ __
_____ __   _____ __

Friday _____

AM Habits   Meals
_____ __   B: _____
_____ __   L: _____
_____ __   D:_____

Mid-Day Habits   Water
_____ __   ☐ ☐ ☐ ☐
_____ __   ☐ ☐ ☐ ☐
_____ __

PM Habits   To Do's
_____ __   _____ __
_____ __   _____ __
_____ __   _____ __

Affirmation:

Saturday _____

AM Habits   Meals
_____ __   B: _____
_____ __   L: _____
_____ __   D:_____

Mid-Day Habits   Water
_____ __   ☐ ☐ ☐ ☐
_____ __   ☐ ☐ ☐ ☐
_____ __

PM Habits   To Do's
_____ __   _____ __
_____ __   _____ __
_____ __   _____ __

Space to Clear Your Mind

♥

Weekly focus:

Sunday _____

AM Habits   Meals
_____ __   B: _____
_____ __   L: _____
_____ __   D:_____

Mid-Day Habits   Water
_____ __   ☐ ☐ ☐ ☐
_____ __   ☐ ☐ ☐ ☐
_____ __

PM Habits   To Do's
_____ __   _____ __
_____ __   _____ __
_____ __   _____ __

Monday _____

AM Habits   Meals
_____ __   B: _____
_____ __   L: _____
_____ __   D:_____

Mid-Day Habits   Water
_____ __   ☐ ☐ ☐ ☐
_____ __   ☐ ☐ ☐ ☐
_____ __

PM Habits   To Do's
_____ __   _____ __
_____ __   _____ __
_____ __   _____ __

Affirmation:

Tuesday _____

AM Habits   Meals
_____ __   B: _____
_____ __   L: _____
_____ __   D:_____

Mid-Day Habits   Water
_____ __   ☐ ☐ ☐ ☐
_____ __   ☐ ☐ ☐ ☐
_____ __

PM Habits   To Do's
_____ __   _____ __
_____ __   _____ __
_____ __   _____ __

Wednesday _____

AM Habits   Meals
_____ __   B: _____
_____ __   L: _____
_____ __   D:_____

Mid-Day Habits   Water
_____ __   ☐ ☐ ☐ ☐
_____ __   ☐ ☐ ☐ ☐
_____ __

PM Habits   To Do's
_____ __   _____ __
_____ __   _____ __
_____ __   _____ __

♥

Monthly intention:

Thursday _____

AM Habits   Meals
_____ __   B: _____
_____ __   L: _____
_____ __   D:_____

Mid-Day Habits   Water
_____ __   ☐ ☐ ☐ ☐
_____ __   ☐ ☐ ☐ ☐
_____ __

PM Habits   To Do's
_____ __   _____ __
_____ __   _____ __
_____ __   _____ __

Friday _____

AM Habits   Meals
_____ __   B: _____
_____ __   L: _____
_____ __   D:_____

Mid-Day Habits   Water
_____ __   ☐ ☐ ☐ ☐
_____ __   ☐ ☐ ☐ ☐
_____ __

PM Habits   To Do's
_____ __   _____ __
_____ __   _____ __
_____ __   _____ __

Affirmation:

Saturday _____   Space to Clear Your Mind

AM Habits   Meals
_____ __   B: _____
_____ __   L: _____
_____ __   D:_____

Mid-Day Habits   Water
_____ __   ☐ ☐ ☐ ☐
_____ __   ☐ ☐ ☐ ☐
_____ __

PM Habits   To Do's
_____ __   _____ __
_____ __   _____ __
_____ __   _____ __

Weekly focus:

Sunday _____

AM Habits	Meals
_____ __	B: _____
_____ __	L: _____
_____ __	D:_____

Mid-Day Habits	Water
_____ __	☐ ☐ ☐ ☐
_____ __	☐ ☐ ☐ ☐
_____ __	

PM Habits	To Do's
_____ __	_____ __
_____ __	_____ __
_____ __	_____ __

Monday _____

AM Habits	Meals
_____ __	B: _____
_____ __	L: _____
_____ __	D:_____

Mid-Day Habits	Water
_____ __	☐ ☐ ☐ ☐
_____ __	☐ ☐ ☐ ☐
_____ __	

PM Habits	To Do's
_____ __	_____ __
_____ __	_____ __
_____ __	_____ __

Affirmation:

Tuesday _____

AM Habits	Meals
_____ __	B: _____
_____ __	L: _____
_____ __	D:_____

Mid-Day Habits	Water
_____ __	☐ ☐ ☐ ☐
_____ __	☐ ☐ ☐ ☐
_____ __	

PM Habits	To Do's
_____ __	_____ __
_____ __	_____ __
_____ __	_____ __

Wednesday _____

AM Habits	Meals
_____ __	B: _____
_____ __	L: _____
_____ __	D:_____

Mid-Day Habits	Water
_____ __	☐ ☐ ☐ ☐
_____ __	☐ ☐ ☐ ☐
_____ __	

PM Habits	To Do's
_____ __	_____ __
_____ __	_____ __
_____ __	_____ __

♥

Monthly intention:

Thursday _____

AM Habits   Meals
_____ __   B: _____
_____ __   L: _____
_____ __   D:_____

Mid-Day Habits   Water
_____ __   ☐ ☐ ☐ ☐
_____ __   ☐ ☐ ☐ ☐
_____ __

PM Habits   To Do's
_____ __   _____ __
_____ __   _____ __
_____ __   _____ __

Friday _____

AM Habits   Meals
_____ __   B: _____
_____ __   L: _____
_____ __   D:_____

Mid-Day Habits   Water
_____ __   ☐ ☐ ☐ ☐
_____ __   ☐ ☐ ☐ ☐
_____ __

PM Habits   To Do's
_____ __   _____ __
_____ __   _____ __
_____ __   _____ __

Affirmation:

Saturday _____

AM Habits   Meals
_____ __   B: _____
_____ __   L: _____
_____ __   D:_____

Mid-Day Habits   Water
_____ __   ☐ ☐ ☐ ☐
_____ __   ☐ ☐ ☐ ☐

PM Habits   To Do's
_____ __   _____ __
_____ __   _____ __
_____ __   _____ __

Space to Clear Your Mind

Weekly focus:

Sunday _____

AM Habits
_____ __
_____ __
_____ __

Meals
B: _____
L: _____
D: _____

Mid-Day Habits
_____ __
_____ __
_____ __

Water
☐ ☐ ☐ ☐
☐ ☐ ☐ ☐

PM Habits
_____ __
_____ __
_____ __

To Do's
_____ __
_____ __
_____ __

Monday _____

AM Habits
_____ __
_____ __
_____ __

Meals
B: _____
L: _____
D: _____

Mid-Day Habits
_____ __
_____ __
_____ __

Water
☐ ☐ ☐ ☐
☐ ☐ ☐ ☐

PM Habits
_____ __
_____ __
_____ __

To Do's
_____ __
_____ __
_____ __

Affirmation:

Tuesday _____

AM Habits
_____ __
_____ __
_____ __

Meals
B: _____
L: _____
D: _____

Mid-Day Habits
_____ __
_____ __

Water
☐ ☐ ☐ ☐
☐ ☐ ☐ ☐

PM Habits
_____ __
_____ __
_____ __

To Do's
_____ __
_____ __
_____ __

Wednesday _____

AM Habits
_____ __
_____ __
_____ __

Meals
B: _____
L: _____
D: _____

Mid-Day Habits
_____ __
_____ __

Water
☐ ☐ ☐ ☐
☐ ☐ ☐ ☐

PM Habits
_____ __
_____ __
_____ __

To Do's
_____ __
_____ __
_____ __

♥

Monthly intention:

Thursday _____

AM Habits   Meals
_____ __   B: _____
_____ __   L: _____
_____ __   D:_____

Mid-Day Habits   Water
_____ __   ☐ ☐ ☐ ☐
_____ __   ☐ ☐ ☐ ☐
_____ __

PM Habits   To Do's
_____ __   _____ __
_____ __   _____ __
_____ __   _____ __

Friday _____

AM Habits   Meals
_____ __   B: _____
_____ __   L: _____
_____ __   D:_____

Mid-Day Habits   Water
_____ __   ☐ ☐ ☐ ☐
_____ __   ☐ ☐ ☐ ☐
_____ __

PM Habits   To Do's
_____ __   _____ __
_____ __   _____ __
_____ __   _____ __

Affirmation:

Saturday _____

AM Habits   Meals
_____ __   B: _____
_____ __   L: _____
_____ __   D:_____

Mid-Day Habits   Water
_____ __   ☐ ☐ ☐ ☐
_____ __   ☐ ☐ ☐ ☐
_____ __

PM Habits   To Do's
_____ __   _____ __
_____ __   _____ __
_____ __   _____ __

Space to Clear Your Mind

Weekly focus:

Sunday _____

AM Habits	Meals
_____ __	B: _____
_____ __	L: _____
_____ __	D:_____

Mid-Day Habits	Water
_____ __	☐ ☐ ☐ ☐
_____ __	☐ ☐ ☐ ☐
_____ __	

PM Habits	To Do's
_____ __	_____ __
_____ __	_____ __
_____ __	_____ __

Monday _____

AM Habits	Meals
_____ __	B: _____
_____ __	L: _____
_____ __	D:_____

Mid-Day Habits	Water
_____ __	☐ ☐ ☐ ☐
_____ __	☐ ☐ ☐ ☐
_____ __	

PM Habits	To Do's
_____ __	_____ __
_____ __	_____ __
_____ __	_____ __

Affirmation:

Tuesday _____

AM Habits	Meals
_____ __	B: _____
_____ __	L: _____
_____ __	D:_____

Mid-Day Habits	Water
_____ __	☐ ☐ ☐ ☐
_____ __	☐ ☐ ☐ ☐
_____ __	

PM Habits	To Do's
_____ __	_____ __
_____ __	_____ __
_____ __	_____ __

Wednesday _____

AM Habits	Meals
_____ __	B: _____
_____ __	L: _____
_____ __	D:_____

Mid-Day Habits	Water
_____ __	☐ ☐ ☐ ☐
_____ __	☐ ☐ ☐ ☐
_____ __	

PM Habits	To Do's
_____ __	_____ __
_____ __	_____ __
_____ __	_____ __

Monthly intention:

Thursday _____

AM Habits | Meals
_____ __ | B: _____
_____ __ | L: _____
_____ __ | D:_____

Mid-Day Habits | Water
_____ __ | ☐ ☐ ☐ ☐
_____ __ | ☐ ☐ ☐ ☐
_____ __ |

PM Habits | To Do's
_____ __ | _____ __
_____ __ | _____ __
_____ __ | _____ __

Friday _____

AM Habits | Meals
_____ __ | B: _____
_____ __ | L: _____
_____ __ | D:_____

Mid-Day Habits | Water
_____ __ | ☐ ☐ ☐ ☐
_____ __ | ☐ ☐ ☐ ☐
_____ __ |

PM Habits | To Do's
_____ __ | _____ __
_____ __ | _____ __
_____ __ | _____ __

Affirmation:

Saturday _____

AM Habits | Meals
_____ __ | B: _____
_____ __ | L: _____
_____ __ | D:_____

Mid-Day Habits | Water
_____ __ | ☐ ☐ ☐ ☐
_____ __ | ☐ ☐ ☐ ☐
_____ __ |

PM Habits | To Do's
_____ __ | _____ __
_____ __ | _____ __
_____ __ | _____ __

Space to Clear Your Mind

♥

Weekly focus:

Sunday _____

AM Habits   Meals
_____ __   B: _____
_____ __   L: _____
_____ __   D:_____

Mid-Day Habits   Water
_____ __   ☐ ☐ ☐ ☐
_____ __   ☐ ☐ ☐ ☐
_____ __

PM Habits   To Do's
_____ __   _____ __
_____ __   _____ __
_____ __   _____ __

Monday _____

AM Habits   Meals
_____ __   B: _____
_____ __   L: _____
_____ __   D:_____

Mid-Day Habits   Water
_____ __   ☐ ☐ ☐ ☐
_____ __   ☐ ☐ ☐ ☐
_____ __

PM Habits   To Do's
_____ __   _____ __
_____ __   _____ __
_____ __   _____ __

Affirmation:

Tuesday _____

AM Habits   Meals
_____ __   B: _____
_____ __   L: _____
_____ __   D:_____

Mid-Day Habits   Water
_____ __   ☐ ☐ ☐ ☐
_____ __   ☐ ☐ ☐ ☐
_____ __

PM Habits   To Do's
_____ __   _____ __
_____ __   _____ __
_____ __   _____ __

Wednesday _____

AM Habits   Meals
_____ __   B: _____
_____ __   L: _____
_____ __   D:_____

Mid-Day Habits   Water
_____ __   ☐ ☐ ☐ ☐
_____ __   ☐ ☐ ☐ ☐
_____ __

PM Habits   To Do's
_____ __   _____ __
_____ __   _____ __
_____ __   _____ __

Monthly intention:

Thursday _____

AM Habits   Meals
_____ __   B: _____
_____ __   L: _____
_____ __   D:_____

Mid-Day Habits   Water
_____ __   ☐ ☐ ☐ ☐
_____ __   ☐ ☐ ☐ ☐
_____ __

PM Habits   To Do's
_____ __   _____ __
_____ __   _____ __
_____ __   _____ __

Friday _____

AM Habits   Meals
_____ __   B: _____
_____ __   L: _____
_____ __   D:_____

Mid-Day Habits   Water
_____ __   ☐ ☐ ☐ ☐
_____ __   ☐ ☐ ☐ ☐
_____ __

PM Habits   To Do's
_____ __   _____ __
_____ __   _____ __
_____ __   _____ __

Affirmation:

Saturday _____   Space to Clear Your Mind

AM Habits   Meals
_____ __   B: _____
_____ __   L: _____
_____ __   D:_____

Mid-Day Habits   Water
_____ __   ☐ ☐ ☐ ☐
_____ __   ☐ ☐ ☐ ☐
_____ __

PM Habits   To Do's
_____ __   _____ __
_____ __   _____ __
_____ __   _____ __

Weekly focus:

Sunday _____

AM Habits	Meals
_____ __	B: _____
_____ __	L: _____
_____ __	D: _____

Mid-Day Habits	Water
_____ _	☐ ☐ ☐ ☐
_____ _	☐ ☐ ☐ ☐
_____ _	

PM Habits	To Do's
_____ __	_____ __
_____ __	_____ __
_____ __	_____ __

Monday _____

AM Habits	Meals
_____ __	B: _____
_____ __	L: _____
_____ __	D: _____

Mid-Day Habits	Water
_____ _	☐ ☐ ☐ ☐
_____ _	☐ ☐ ☐ ☐
_____ _	

PM Habits	To Do's
_____ __	_____ __
_____ __	_____ __
_____ __	_____ __

Affirmation:

Tuesday _____

AM Habits	Meals
_____ __	B: _____
_____ __	L: _____
_____ __	D: _____

Mid-Day Habits	Water
_____ _	☐ ☐ ☐ ☐
_____ _	☐ ☐ ☐ ☐
_____ _	

PM Habits	To Do's
_____ __	_____ __
_____ __	_____ __
_____ __	_____ __

Wednesday _____

AM Habits	Meals
_____ __	B: _____
_____ __	L: _____
_____ __	D: _____

Mid-Day Habits	Water
_____ _	☐ ☐ ☐ ☐
_____ _	☐ ☐ ☐ ☐
_____ _	

PM Habits	To Do's
_____ __	_____ __
_____ __	_____ __
_____ __	_____ __

Monthly intention:

Thursday _____

AM Habits   Meals
_____ __   B: _____
_____ __   L: _____
_____ __   D: _____

Mid-Day Habits   Water
_____ __   ☐ ☐ ☐ ☐
_____ __   ☐ ☐ ☐ ☐
_____ __

PM Habits   To Do's
_____ __   _____ __
_____ __   _____ __
_____ __   _____ __

Friday _____

AM Habits   Meals
_____ __   B: _____
_____ __   L: _____
_____ __   D: _____

Mid-Day Habits   Water
_____ __   ☐ ☐ ☐ ☐
_____ __   ☐ ☐ ☐ ☐
_____ __

PM Habits   To Do's
_____ __   _____ __
_____ __   _____ __
_____ __   _____ __

Affirmation:

Saturday _____

AM Habits   Meals
_____ __   B: _____
_____ __   L: _____
_____ __   D: _____

Mid-Day Habits   Water
_____ __   ☐ ☐ ☐ ☐
_____ __   ☐ ☐ ☐ ☐
_____ __

PM Habits   To Do's
_____ __   _____ __
_____ __   _____ __
_____ __   _____ __

Space to Clear Your Mind

Weekly focus:

Sunday _____

AM Habits   Meals
_____ __ B: _____
_____ __ L: _____
_____ __ D:_____

Mid-Day Habits Water
_____ __ ☐ ☐ ☐ ☐
_____ __ ☐ ☐ ☐ ☐
_____ __

PM Habits   To Do's
_____ __ _____ __
_____ __ _____ __
_____ __ _____ __

Monday _____

AM Habits   Meals
_____ __ B: _____
_____ __ L: _____
_____ __ D:_____

Mid-Day Habits Water
_____ __ ☐ ☐ ☐ ☐
_____ __ ☐ ☐ ☐ ☐
_____ __

PM Habits   To Do's
_____ __ _____ __
_____ __ _____ __
_____ __ _____ __

Affirmation:

Tuesday _____

AM Habits   Meals
_____ __ B: _____
_____ __ L: _____
_____ __ D:_____

Mid-Day Habits Water
_____ __ ☐ ☐ ☐ ☐
_____ __ ☐ ☐ ☐ ☐
_____ __

PM Habits   To Do's
_____ __ _____ __
_____ __ _____ __
_____ __ _____ __

Wednesday _____

AM Habits   Meals
_____ __ B: _____
_____ __ L: _____
_____ __ D:_____

Mid-Day Habits Water
_____ __ ☐ ☐ ☐ ☐
_____ __ ☐ ☐ ☐ ☐
_____ __

PM Habits   To Do's
_____ __ _____ __
_____ __ _____ __
_____ __ _____ __

Monthly intention:

Thursday _____

AM Habits   Meals
_____ __   B: _____
_____ __   L: _____
_____ __   D:_____

Mid-Day Habits   Water
_____ __   ☐ ☐ ☐ ☐
_____ __   ☐ ☐ ☐ ☐
_____ __

PM Habits   To Do's
_____ __   _____ __
_____ __   _____ __
_____ __   _____ __

Friday _____

AM Habits   Meals
_____ __   B: _____
_____ __   L: _____
_____ __   D:_____

Mid-Day Habits   Water
_____ __   ☐ ☐ ☐ ☐
_____ __   ☐ ☐ ☐ ☐
_____ __

PM Habits   To Do's
_____ __   _____ __
_____ __   _____ __
_____ __   _____ __

Affirmation:

Saturday _____

AM Habits   Meals
_____ __   B: _____
_____ __   L: _____
_____ __   D:_____

Mid-Day Habits   Water
_____ __   ☐ ☐ ☐ ☐
_____ __   ☐ ☐ ☐ ☐
_____ __

PM Habits   To Do's
_____ __   _____ __
_____ __   _____ __
_____ __   _____ __

Space to Clear Your Mind

Weekly focus:

Sunday _____

AM Habits   Meals
_____ __   B: _____
_____ __   L: _____
_____ __   D: _____

Mid-Day Habits   Water
_____ __   ☐ ☐ ☐ ☐
_____ __   ☐ ☐ ☐ ☐
_____ __

PM Habits   To Do's
_____ __   _____ __
_____ __   _____ __
_____ __   _____ __

Monday _____

AM Habits   Meals
_____ __   B: _____
_____ __   L: _____
_____ __   D: _____

Mid-Day Habits   Water
_____ __   ☐ ☐ ☐ ☐
_____ __   ☐ ☐ ☐ ☐
_____ __

PM Habits   To Do's
_____ __   _____ __
_____ __   _____ __
_____ __   _____ __

Affirmation:

Tuesday _____

AM Habits   Meals
_____ __   B: _____
_____ __   L: _____
_____ __   D: _____

Mid-Day Habits   Water
_____ __   ☐ ☐ ☐ ☐
_____ __   ☐ ☐ ☐ ☐
_____ __

PM Habits   To Do's
_____ __   _____ __
_____ __   _____ __
_____ __   _____ __

Wednesday _____

AM Habits   Meals
_____ __   B: _____
_____ __   L: _____
_____ __   D: _____

Mid-Day Habits   Water
_____ __   ☐ ☐ ☐ ☐
_____ __   ☐ ☐ ☐ ☐
_____ __

PM Habits   To Do's
_____ __   _____ __
_____ __   _____ __
_____ __   _____ __

Monthly intention:

Thursday _____

AM Habits | Meals
_____ __ | B: _____
_____ __ | L: _____
_____ __ | D:_____

Mid-Day Habits | Water
_____ __ | ☐ ☐ ☐ ☐
_____ __ | ☐ ☐ ☐ ☐
_____ __ |

PM Habits | To Do's
_____ __ | _____ __
_____ __ | _____ __
_____ __ | _____ __

Friday _____

AM Habits | Meals
_____ __ | B: _____
_____ __ | L: _____
_____ __ | D:_____

Mid-Day Habits | Water
_____ __ | ☐ ☐ ☐ ☐
_____ __ | ☐ ☐ ☐ ☐
_____ __ |

PM Habits | To Do's
_____ __ | _____ __
_____ __ | _____ __
_____ __ | _____ __

Affirmation:

Saturday _____

AM Habits | Meals
_____ __ | B: _____
_____ __ | L: _____
_____ __ | D:_____

Mid-Day Habits | Water
_____ __ | ☐ ☐ ☐ ☐
_____ __ | ☐ ☐ ☐ ☐
_____ __ |

PM Habits | To Do's
_____ __ | _____ __
_____ __ | _____ __
_____ __ | _____ __

Space to Clear Your Mind

Weekly focus:

Sunday _____

AM Habits

_____ __
_____ __
_____ __

Meals

B: _____
L: _____
D:_____

Mid-Day Habits

_____ __
_____ __
_____ __

Water

☐ ☐ ☐ ☐
☐ ☐ ☐ ☐

PM Habits

_____ __
_____ __
_____ __

To Do's

_____ __
_____ __
_____ __

Monday _____

AM Habits

_____ __
_____ __
_____ __

Meals

B: _____
L: _____
D:_____

Mid-Day Habits

_____ __
_____ __
_____ __

Water

☐ ☐ ☐ ☐
☐ ☐ ☐ ☐

PM Habits

_____ __
_____ __
_____ __

To Do's

_____ __
_____ __
_____ __

Affirmation:

Tuesday _____

AM Habits

_____ __
_____ __
_____ __

Meals

B: _____
L: _____
D:_____

Mid-Day Habits

_____ __
_____ __
_____ __

Water

☐ ☐ ☐ ☐
☐ ☐ ☐ ☐

PM Habits

_____ __
_____ __
_____ __

To Do's

_____ __
_____ __
_____ __

Wednesday _____

AM Habits

_____ __
_____ __
_____ __

Meals

B: _____
L: _____
D:_____

Mid-Day Habits

_____ __
_____ __
_____ __

Water

☐ ☐ ☐ ☐
☐ ☐ ☐ ☐

PM Habits

_____ __
_____ __
_____ __

To Do's

_____ __
_____ __
_____ __

Monthly intention:

Thursday _____

AM Habits   Meals
_____ __   B: _____
_____ __   L: _____
_____ __   D: _____

Mid-Day Habits   Water
_____ __   ☐ ☐ ☐ ☐
_____ __   ☐ ☐ ☐ ☐
_____ __

PM Habits   To Do's
_____ __   _____ __
_____ __   _____ __
_____ __   _____ __

Friday _____

AM Habits   Meals
_____ __   B: _____
_____ __   L: _____
_____ __   D: _____

Mid-Day Habits   Water
_____ __   ☐ ☐ ☐ ☐
_____ __   ☐ ☐ ☐ ☐
_____ __

PM Habits   To Do's
_____ __   _____ __
_____ __   _____ __
_____ __   _____ __

Affirmation:

Saturday _____   Space to Clear Your Mind

AM Habits   Meals
_____ __   B: _____
_____ __   L: _____
_____ __   D: _____

Mid-Day Habits   Water
_____ __   ☐ ☐ ☐ ☐
_____ __   ☐ ☐ ☐ ☐
_____ __

PM Habits   To Do's
_____ __   _____ __
_____ __   _____ __
_____ __   _____ __

Weekly focus:

Sunday _____

AM Habits | Meals
_____ __ | B: _____
_____ __ | L: _____
_____ __ | D:_____

Mid-Day Habits | Water
_____ __ | ☐ ☐ ☐ ☐
_____ __ | ☐ ☐ ☐ ☐
_____ __ |

PM Habits | To Do's
_____ __ | _____ __
_____ __ | _____ __
_____ __ | _____ __

Monday _____

AM Habits | Meals
_____ __ | B: _____
_____ __ | L: _____
_____ __ | D:_____

Mid-Day Habits | Water
_____ __ | ☐ ☐ ☐ ☐
_____ __ | ☐ ☐ ☐ ☐
_____ __ |

PM Habits | To Do's
_____ __ | _____ __
_____ __ | _____ __
_____ __ | _____ __

Affirmation:

Tuesday _____

AM Habits | Meals
_____ __ | B: _____
_____ __ | L: _____
_____ __ | D:_____

Mid-Day Habits | Water
_____ __ | ☐ ☐ ☐ ☐
_____ __ | ☐ ☐ ☐ ☐
_____ __ |

PM Habits | To Do's
_____ __ | _____ __
_____ __ | _____ __
_____ __ | _____ __

Wednesday _____

AM Habits | Meals
_____ __ | B: _____
_____ __ | L: _____
_____ __ | D:_____

Mid-Day Habits | Water
_____ __ | ☐ ☐ ☐ ☐
_____ __ | ☐ ☐ ☐ ☐
_____ __ |

PM Habits | To Do's
_____ __ | _____ __
_____ __ | _____ __
_____ __ | _____ __

Monthly intention:

Thursday _____

AM Habits	Meals
_____ __	B: _____
_____ __	L: _____
_____ __	D: _____

Mid-Day Habits	Water
_____ __	☐ ☐ ☐ ☐
_____ __	☐ ☐ ☐ ☐
_____ __	

PM Habits	To Do's
_____ __	_____ __
_____ __	_____ __
_____ __	_____ __

Friday _____

AM Habits	Meals
_____ __	B: _____
_____ __	L: _____
_____ __	D: _____

Mid-Day Habits	Water
_____ __	☐ ☐ ☐ ☐
_____ __	☐ ☐ ☐ ☐
_____ __	

PM Habits	To Do's
_____ __	_____ __
_____ __	_____ __
_____ __	_____ __

Affirmation:

Saturday _____

AM Habits	Meals
_____ __	B: _____
_____ __	L: _____
_____ __	D: _____

Mid-Day Habits	Water
_____ __	☐ ☐ ☐ ☐
_____ __	☐ ☐ ☐ ☐
_____ __	

PM Habits	To Do's
_____ __	_____ __
_____ __	_____ __
_____ __	_____ __

Space to Clear Your Mind

Weekly focus:

Sunday _____

AM Habits   Meals
_____ __   B: _____
_____ __   L: _____
_____ __   D: _____

Mid-Day Habits   Water
_____ __   ☐ ☐ ☐ ☐
_____ __   ☐ ☐ ☐ ☐
_____ __

PM Habits   To Do's
_____ __   _____ __
_____ __   _____ __
_____ __   _____ __

Monday _____

AM Habits   Meals
_____ __   B: _____
_____ __   L: _____
_____ __   D: _____

Mid-Day Habits   Water
_____ __   ☐ ☐ ☐ ☐
_____ __   ☐ ☐ ☐ ☐
_____ __

PM Habits   To Do's
_____ __   _____ __
_____ __   _____ __
_____ __   _____ __

Affirmation:

Tuesday _____

AM Habits   Meals
_____ __   B: _____
_____ __   L: _____
_____ __   D: _____

Mid-Day Habits   Water
_____ __   ☐ ☐ ☐ ☐
_____ __   ☐ ☐ ☐ ☐
_____ __

PM Habits   To Do's
_____ __   _____ __
_____ __   _____ __
_____ __   _____ __

Wednesday _____

AM Habits   Meals
_____ __   B: _____
_____ __   L: _____
_____ __   D: _____

Mid-Day Habits   Water
_____ __   ☐ ☐ ☐ ☐
_____ __   ☐ ☐ ☐ ☐
_____ __

PM Habits   To Do's
_____ __   _____ __
_____ __   _____ __
_____ __   _____ __

♥

Monthly intention:

Thursday _____

AM Habits   Meals
_____ __   B: _____
_____ __   L: _____
_____ __   D:_____

Mid-Day Habits   Water
_____ __   ☐ ☐ ☐ ☐
_____ __   ☐ ☐ ☐ ☐
_____ __

PM Habits   To Do's
_____ __   _____ __
_____ __   _____ __
_____ __   _____ __

Friday _____

AM Habits   Meals
_____ __   B: _____
_____ __   L: _____
_____ __   D:_____

Mid-Day Habits   Water
_____ __   ☐ ☐ ☐ ☐
_____ __   ☐ ☐ ☐ ☐
_____ __

PM Habits   To Do's
_____ __   _____ __
_____ __   _____ __
_____ __   _____ __

Affirmation:

Saturday _____

AM Habits   Meals
_____ __   B: _____
_____ __   L: _____
_____ __   D:_____

Mid-Day Habits   Water
_____ __   ☐ ☐ ☐ ☐
_____ __   ☐ ☐ ☐ ☐
_____ __

PM Habits   To Do's
_____ __   _____ __
_____ __   _____ __
_____ __   _____ __

Space to Clear Your Mind

Part 8: Close the year

As the days grow colder and shorter, it's a perfect time to go within.

Thinking about a new year and making plans for how you want to harness the fresh energy is exciting.

But taking this time to first connect in is important to continue living with intention and soul.

These short questions will also help you absorb the year's lessons and blessings to embody the growth you've experienced.

So grab a cup of tea or hot chocolate, light a candle, and dive in.

What was this the year of?

_____

_____

_____

_____

_____

_____

_____

_____

_____

_____

What was your biggest life lesson?

_____

_____

_____

_____

_____

_____

_____

_____

_____

_____

If you could deliver a message to the January version of you, what would it be?

_____

_____

_____

_____

_____

_____

_____

_____

_____

_____

_____

What do you want next year to be about?

_____

_____

_____

_____

_____

_____

_____

_____

_____

_____

_____

What are one or two things you are ready to focus on and create for yourself?

_____

_____

_____

_____

_____

_____

_____

_____

_____

_____

_____

_____

Connect to the next December version of you who is fulfilled, abundant, successful and happy. What message does she have for you?

_____

_____

_____

_____

_____

_____

_____

_____

_____

_____

_____

_____

_____

_____

_____

_____

_____

_____

_____

_____

_____

_____

_____

_____

_____

*Did you enjoy this journal? Order one for next year at
SoulScrollJournals.com! See you next year!*

Notes and reflections

All of life is a series of cycles.

Inhales followed by exhales. Happiness followed by sadness. Growth followed by loss. Decay followed by regeneration.

The more we can embrace these cycles and lean into them rather than fight them or feel like something is wrong with us for experiencing them, the more soulful and happy our lives become.

All through the years, we die so many little deaths, saying good-bye to outdated versions of ourselves, and sometimes the people and places that go along with them.

We are also born again countless times. Each new day, each new moment, is a chance to begin again. Start fresh. Begin something new. Give ourselves the gift of a fresh chance.

We're not alive to be perfect, but to revel into the cracks of imperfection. To turn what's broken into something beautiful, the place where we make ourselves whole.

The holy contradiction in life is that we are perfectly imperfect. Crazy and sane. Divinely guided yet forever uncertain.

Rather than making sense of the mysteries, a soulful life demands that we celebrate them. Accepting life and ourselves exactly as they are.

And in the peace of that acceptance, we so easily and gracefully blossom into the person we've always known we could be. Today, we celebrate the extraordinarily unique being that is you.

The end!

Thank you so much for choosing Soul Scroll Journals as a guide through the galaxy of your inner world!

Our mission is to help you understand yourself so you can create a life as unique as you are.

We hope that you now feel more empowered to create a beautiful life of your choosing rather than the one you're programmed for or expected to live.

Please let us know how your experience was!

What's next:

1. Leave a review.

Did you love this journal? Share your thoughts on Amazon.

Reviews are important for helping people decide if this journal will help them create their desired result. Sharing your experiences helps others create happy lives, and happy people will create a better world.

2. Download your bonus gifts at SoulScrollJournals.com/bonuses.

On the website, you'll find an array of free meditations to heal your heart and other resources to know yourself, love yourself and trust yourself to create a life as unique as you are.

About Soul Scroll Journals

Everyone has a dream inside of them they're meant to live. Yet not everyone trusts themselves enough to create this dream and realize their destiny.

This is no small thing. You have a unique combination of gifts, insights and perspectives the world needs. You have something special deep within you that, once discovered, will give your life meaning and beauty.

Yet too many people hold themselves back from embarking on this epic quest of realizing their dreams because they don't believe in themselves. They may be held back by past pain or unsure how to reprogram their minds with loving and encouraging thoughts.

This is why Soul Scroll Journals was born.

Founder Suzanne Heyn's special gift is helping people know, love and understand themselves through asking simple, powerful questions.

Through guided Soul Scroll Journals, Suzanne wants to inspire you to put down your phone and scroll your soul. To discover the vision within and connect to the heartfelt guidance to manifest it, one day at a time, ultimately creating a life as unique as you are.

These journals are your friend and unbiased guide to help you connect to your heart, clarify your dreams and desires, and become the person you were always meant to be — while having a blast along the way.

Find more journals to understand yourself and create a life as unique as you are at SoulScrollJournals.com.

Thank you for choosing us as a guide!

Made in the USA
Coppell, TX
22 August 2022

81862002R00142